PENGUIN BUSINESS

FIVE ENERGIES OF HORRIBLE BOSSES AND
HOW NOT TO BECOME ONE

Recipient of the 2012 Global HR Excellence Award in Leadership, the 2016 Global Coaching Leadership Award, and voted 2020 Executive Coach of the Year in Singapore, Marcel Daane is considered one of the world's authorities in mind-body leadership, a holistic approach to leadership using mindfulness, neuroscience, and body-awareness that inspires a way of being that empowers authenticity, openness, empathy, and trust.

He is the author of his critically acclaimed book *Headstrong Performance: Improve Your Mental Performance with Nutrition, Exercise, and Neuroscience.*

Marcel is a life-long practitioner of martial arts and is the son of a celebrated Political Activist who taught him early on that life has greater meaning when we are of service to others rather than merely to ourselves. This value shines through in everything Marcel has done in his thirty-year professional evolution ranging from serving in the military to developing elite athletes, coaching chronically ill patients, conducting ground-breaking neuro-leadership research, and in his executive coaching work transforming today's top managers into tomorrow's top leaders.

In his free time, Marcel volunteers as a Mental Health & Wellness advocate supporting professionals struggling with mental wellness challenges and loves to spend quality family time with his wife, Ursula, and Daughter, Kilani.

Marcel holds a post-graduate degree in the Neuroscience of Leadership from Middlesex University, an Undergraduate Degree in Complementary Medicine from Charles Sturt University coupled with advanced certifications in Executive Coaching, Fitness, and Sports Performance.

T0150071

Five Energies of Horrible Bosses and How Not to Become One

by

Marcel Daane

BUSINESS

An imprint of Penguin Random House

PENGUIN BUSINESS

USA I Canada I UK I Ireland I Australia
New Zealand I India I South Africa I China I Southeast Asia

Penguin Business is part of the Penguin Random House group of companies
whose addresses can be found at global.penguinrandomhouse.com

Published by Penguin Random House SEA Pte Ltd
9, Changi South Street 3, Level 08-01,
Singapore 486361

First published in Penguin Business by Penguin Random House SEA 2021
Copyright © Marcel Daane 2021

ISBN 9789814954648

www.penguin.sg

Table of Contents

Introduction

Let's face it; the years 2020 and 2021 have to go down as among the weirdest years in modern history. In my mind, these two years will be most remembered in history for the COVID-19 pandemic that infected hundreds of millions of people and killed over four million people worldwide. Not only did this pandemic impact the lives of the people infected and their immediate families, but it impacted the lives of billions of people the moment countries were forced to close their borders, their businesses, their schools, and even confine people to their homes. In a matter of a few days, as the pandemic swept over the globe, it was as if the world went dark in its wake.

Prior to the pandemic, I was living a life blissfully unaware of the carnage about to be unleashed upon us by a single micro-organism. One could say I was living the dream prior to the pandemic. I was living a life of comfort in one of the most exotic cities in the world with my wife and my daughter who love and adore me.

As an author and coach, I considered myself extremely fortunate that I got to spend my days travelling around the world, running leadership conferences for senior leadership teams of multinational companies.

Honestly, I loved my travelling so much that there were days when I would wake up in the morning in the most lavish hotel suite, in some exotic place like Thailand, Dubai, or Hawaii and I would pinch myself to make sure I wasn't dreaming. Not a day would go by where I wouldn't wake up with a smile on my face, thinking I have won the lottery of life. Yes, life was that good.

The year 2020 started off really good for me. I clearly remember having breakfast with my wife and daughter one day in January of 2020, while we were on vacation at a luxury resort in Thailand. As we were sitting on the balcony of our suite, enjoying a mix of local and western dishes, I took a sip of my most exquisite Thai coffee and told my wife how 2020 was going to be my best year yet. For the first time since starting my leadership company, I had bookings lined up till the end of the year which promised some of the best travel experiences, and accompanying that, some incredible revenue as well. Even though there was mention in the news of how the disease was spreading in China, I did not see any reason to worry about whether or not the situation in China would affect me or my business. It seemed like a very isolated issue. The forecast for 2020 was looking great.

Four weeks later, the world turned upside down and all travel plans got cancelled. Sitting at my desk in my home office, I was receiving one email after the other from my clients, all cancelling the bookings for the leadership events that year. In the span of twenty-four hours, I went from having a wonderful outlook for the year to being completely out of work and out of revenue. As the emails rolled in, I could feel my heart sink, while my head was racing, trying to think of how I could salvage my business. I could feel myself going numb as the whole world was rapidly shutting down. Over the span of the next few days, I wandered around the house like a zombie, in my pajamas, trying to make sense of everything that was happening. Just like so many other people in the world at that time, I spent my days in horror, watching the news on television showing the COVID-19 infection rates, hospitalizations, and death toll.

I remember watching on CNN International, how many businesses were suffering and how so many employees were being displaced and laid off from their jobs without any positive prospects in sight. As I was watching that episode, I started thinking about my clients and their companies, and decided to start reaching out to them to see if there was anything I could do to help reduce their suffering. To my surprise, a number of my clients mentioned the challenges that they were facing while trying to pivot into operating virtually. When I asked them what their greatest challenge was, the answer was fairly consistent across the board. 'How do we ensure everybody stay connected with their team-members, despite working virtually and remotely?'

As I sat and thought about that for a while, I decided then and there that there was something I could do to help ease the suffering of my clients. I then reached out to each of them and offered to work with each of their teams on how to keep their spirits up, improve well-being, and build team connectedness despite being in lockdown, and I offered to do this completely free of charge, simply as a means to give back. To my pleasant surprise, most of my clients jumped on the opportunity, and before I know it, I had a full schedule again, albeit without any revenue. Even though I wasn't receiving immediate revenue from my initiative, I felt tremendous satisfaction in that I was contributing to making other people's lives better. Even though I was teaching them how to energize themselves, I too began to feel extremely energized from the work I was doing.

During those days, one of my challenges was to develop the quickest way possible to help teams and individual leaders better manage their own Energy and how to use that Energy to stay connected to their teams, peers, and customers, despite being so far apart from each other. So, I began to explore what would be the best way to help professionals achieve just that.

As months went by conducting many free workshops and coaching sessions for these companies, their leaders, and their teams, a framework slowly started to emerge that not only helped teams manage their Energy better during lockdown, but they even began to notice how using this framework helped them become more productive while working in a virtual environment.

The results for my contacts who practiced this framework became such a game-changer for them that people began to refer clients to me. Before I knew it, I was delivering virtual coaching and training programs in this framework on a full-time basis and making a very decent living in the process. My desire to simply give back and help people get through COVID lockdown turned into an incredible gift for me that I could never have expected. What started off as a year of setbacks, disappointments, and devastation eventually turned out to be one of the best years of my life.

For that reason, I want to share this framework with you as well, hoping it will have the same impact on you and on how you operate as a person, professional, and as a leader. And yet, even though the highlight of this book might be the framework that can help professionals and bosses be more effective, I have written this book from the heart, sharing as much of myself and my experience with Energy in a real and uncensored way.

In Chapter 1 of this book, I share my own bumpy ride in the early years of my life when I struggled with depression and alcoholism and how the introduction to an amazing martial arts master changed my life forever. In Chapter 2, I share how, like so many of my clients, I have struggled to maintain my own Energy as an adult, and how that resulted in me becoming one of the most horrible bosses I have ever known.

In Chapter 3, I use 'the weather' as a metaphor to share some of my experiences as a coach when observing in other companies how the Energy of their leaders shapes the atmosphere inside the company. Chapter 4 explores the three pillars of wisdom in leadership and how accessing and trusting our wisdom is a critical element in effective leadership for every boss. In Chapter 5, I share a four-step approach to help you access greater wisdom in everything you do.

Chapter 6 delves deeper into the research behind Energy, how it's understood in Western and Asian cultures, and how new developments in research technology is helping us create a scientifically sound blend of two. Chapter 7 is the introduction to the Five Energies and how I came about creating the Five Energies Framework. Chapters 8 to 12 explores each of the Energy projections, how the Energy shows up for you in body-mind-action, and offers real-life scenarios to showcase how projecting energies in certain ways can either serve us, or not serve us so well.

In Chapter 13, I invite you to assess your own Energy projection through a ten-scenario questionnaire. Chapter 14 then provides you with a road-map to help you shift your own Energy, but also provides you with a powerful model called N.I.C.E.R. to help you match the Energy of any of your counterparts while also offering a system to help your counterparts shift Energy with you for a more favourable outcome when working with other people.

Finally, in Chapter 15, I share the five fundamental tai chi principles, how they apply to leadership, and how you can use your understanding of the five tai chi principles to help you overcome challenges when practicing the new skills in this book.

As you embark on reading this book, I encourage you to resist the temptation of rushing through the book. Instead, I would like to ask that you take some time at the end of each chapter to reflect on your own learning and perhaps refer back to moments in your own life where you may have had your own experiences with Energy and leadership. Once you get to Chapter Eight and begin exploring each of the energies for yourself in subsequent chapters, I would highly recommend that you pause at each of the chapters and take some time to practice the exercises that are covered in these chapters. Much more than an academic exercise, this framework is meant to align your body and mind through a combination of physical and mental exercises. For these exercises to have the most impact on you, you will need to do some actual practicing. The more you practice, the more these exercises, and therefore this framework, will work for you.

I cannot begin to tell you how excited I am that you are reading my book and that you will be trying out this framework for yourself. I wish you the best of luck as you embark on your own journey with Energy and am really looking forward to the possible positive impact you may have on the people in your life and business.

Chapter 1

A Bumpy Ride

Before I get into my story, I would like to start this book with a disclaimer. I am, by no means, an expert in Energy or Energy healing. I did not spend a great portion of my life living with Tibetan Monks. I also never completed a PhD in the subject matter, or any subject for that matter. I am also not a doctor who specializes in Energy healing. Another thing that I am not is a business or finance guru. I am also not a billionaire who promises to share the secret of financial wealth and independence in this book, nor am I the CEO of a multinational organization.

What I am though is that I am, probably, very much like you. I am a normal—for the most part—human being, who was raised in Western society in a Western educational system, with Western cultural influences. Where I might have you beat is that I have failed more often in my life than I have succeeded, and that includes getting fired from every single job for which I was hired, except for my time in the military. This even includes being fired from my own company which I had founded about fifteen years ago. Looking at all this, it probably doesn't look like I have much of a track record that will give me a lot of credibility in this subject. And yet, here we are.

This book has not been written from the perspective of an expert, or a teacher. Instead, I want to share with you how life changed for the better for me when I learned to be consciously aware of how I project Energy and the impact it has had on my relationships, in how I conduct my work, and on my life. So, this is book is not written from a vantage point of academic knowledge, but is simply written from a perspective of life experience.

It might come as a surprise to you, but it's only been about ten years or so that I have been incorporating Energy work, and in particular conscious Energy projection, into my own life and my coaching. When I, finally—after many ups and downs—learned to appreciate the positive power of Energy, it felt like a veil was lifted from how I viewed my world and my circumstances. The clarity that was presented to me was life changing and I want to share with you how, through those many ups and downs, this awareness helped me live a more fulfilled and happy life in both business and at home with the hope that it will help you in your work and life.

Now that we have that out of the way, let's go back to the beginning. Where does my fascination with Energy work, Energy projection, and leadership come from? Well, my fascination with Energy work goes way back to when I was living in New Zealand as a Dutch immigrant child during the first seven years of my life. I attended my first karate class when I was six in 1972. The year before Bruce Lee passed away. Why is that significant? Well, because studying martial arts in the 1970s was significantly different than it is today. Especially for a six-year-old. In that era, there were no kids' classes for martial arts. If you were a kid wanting to learn martial arts, you had to endure the training intensity of an adult training program. I do have to be honest, taking karate classes wasn't my idea at all. It was actually my mom's idea.

You see, my mom was a very special individual. Even though she was a regular mom by day, by night, she was a prominent exiled South African political activist fighting the White Supremacist Apartheid Regime at that time. My mom made a promise to herself that her kids would grow up to be warriors, like she was. Warrior kids who would make a stand for what's right and fair in this world, who would rise up against injustice, and who would be prepared to fight on behalf of the many oppressed people in this world who could not fight for themselves.

Unfortunately for me, I was the farthest thing away from being a warrior kid. Growing up, I was a very sensitive kid. Like pretty much every other small child, I was extremely playful, fun-loving, imaginative, and carefree, while also being extremely empathetic. For as long as I can remember, I always had this natural connection with the Energy that all living beings project. No matter if it was a human being, a dog, an insect, or a plant, I could feel a deep connection with all of them.

Thinking back, I believe that spending my formative years in such a magical land as New Zealand really deepened my connection with the natural world. *If you have never visited New Zealand before, just watch the movie Lord of the Rings and you'll get what I mean.* I spent most of my days playing and exploring in nature. I would spend my time climbing trees, exploring forests, and even wading through rivers without any worry in the world. And with every day that I was immersed in nature, I developed an intense sensitivity to the Energy of the natural world. I could never place my finger on how I felt, but generally this connection would show up to me in the form of a rush of Energy that would envelope my entire body when in the presence of any living being. The best way to describe the feeling is that it is like standing in the surf of the ocean and feeling a wave come over me. Some waves are small and harmless, others were like rolling waves that would feel like fun as they gently picked me up off the ground and put me back down. Some waves, however, were a lot more aggressive and scarier. Those waves of Energy would feel like big angry waves that would come crushing down on top of me.

Unfortunately for me, my mom's anger and determination while fighting a foreign government were like the angry waves to me, which meant that I spent most of my time at home being withdrawn. My family interpreted my withdrawn nature as me being a shy kid, when in fact, I was living in constant fear, feeling completely overwhelmed by the angry waves of Energy in our household. In my withdrawn state, I became a chronic nail-biter, and resorted to soothing myself with comfort food. Not exactly an image of a warrior who stands up against injustice and fights for the weak, right? Instead, I became exactly the opposite of a warrior. I became that chubby, shy kid who didn't have a lot of confidence, who didn't have a lot of friends, and who wasn't even capable of standing up to a cookie.

Now, don't get me wrong. My mom loved us a lot, and there was nothing she wouldn't have done to fight for the safety and well-being of her kids. So, from her perspective, there was nothing she was doing wrong as a parent. She simply was not aware of the effect that her assertive Energy had on at least one of her kids. So, my mom decided that when I was five or six years old, I needed more discipline and training to create the warrior that she wanted to see in all of us. For that reason, I ended up being one of the only children in New Zealand to start practicing karate. And at the age of six, I was actually featured in the newspaper as the youngest orange belt in New Zealand.

Funny enough, my mom's plan worked somewhat. Even though I was this sensitive and withdrawn kid at home, I discovered that martial arts somehow ignited the same Energy in me that I would experience when being in nature, despite being in a world of grown-ups. The countless hours and thousands of repetitions of punches, kicks, stances, and forms never fatigued me, but instead energized me, and with it, energised my confidence. And just like I experienced in nature, the dojo became a place where I felt I could be free to have fun, explore myself, and challenge my physical and mental abilities as a martial artist.

Over the years that followed, my family and I moved back to the Netherlands. Even though the Netherlands is a very pretty country, we moved to a city where I no longer could feel that same connection with nature that I had when I lived in New Zealand. Very soon, my depressed, overweight, and nail-biting self would begin to show up again. In every aspect of my life, except when I was practicing martial arts. Luckily, there was a Karate dojo in my neighbourhood, which became a new martial arts home for me.

At one point, when I was fourteen years old, my parents became so concerned about me that they decided to make me see a psychiatrist who diagnosed me as having severe clinical depression and anxiety. One thing I am grateful for to my mom till today is that she told me that she too suffered from depression and had been using meditation for years to help keep her depression at bay. My mom was the first person to teach me how to meditate, and little did she know, but that was probably the greatest gift she has ever given me because it's something I use even today to keep my depression under control.

One day, at my dojo, my teacher was talking about one of his favourite books, Sun Tzu's *The Art of War*. I listened in fascination as my teacher was describing how this book had made such an impact on how he trained, competed, and lived his life. Immediately, I hopped on my bicycle and raced to the nearest library. To my delight, I found one copy of the book in a section that I had never thought of exploring before, Eastern philosophy. There were so many fascinating books like Miyamoto Musashi's *The Book of Five Rings*, Lau Tzu's *Tao Te Ching*, and many more. Just looking at the covers of those books, I could feel an Energy that drew me to them as if they were saying, 'Read Me', and that I did. Inspired by Eastern philosophy texts and numerous books on the way of the warrior, I found myself being drawn to how the ancient masters of the martial arts would use meditation to push their bodies to develop incredible reflexes, speed, and power, and I became determined to follow their example in my own training.

I, then, started to combine mindfulness training with my own martial arts practice and the results were profound for me. Both inside and outside the dojo, I noticed that I was becoming much more aware of my presence in every situation. I noticed how my mental focus and processing speed improved. It was as if the world started to slow down for me, which gave me space to observe and think about how to react in different situations. For the first time in my life, I could see the waves of Energy, even the angry waves, coming at me at a seemingly slower and much less overwhelming pace. Slowly but surely, I felt myself become more centred and confident. My mood at home and everywhere else began to change. I could feel my depression being lifted from me as if a heavy weight was being removed from my body. This was not only figuratively, but also literally, as I also started to lose weight. Within a few years, I transformed myself from a clinically depressed, overwhelmed, and overweight kid into a strong, confident, and fit young man, not only at the dojo, but also at home.

By the age of eighteen, after I graduated high school, I decided to continue my warrior way and enlisted in the Dutch Royal Navy, not knowing that, once again, I was going to be overwhelmed by the crashing energy waves, similar to what I experienced at home, but this time a thousand times more intense.

From the moment I stepped out of the bus and set foot on the military base to begin my basic training, I could feel the rush of intense energy come over me, as the drill-sergeant approached me, yelling and screaming. His aggressive energy hit me like a baseball bat and immediately, I could feel every ounce of confidence that I had built up in the dojo flow out of my body. In an instant, I could feel myself once again withdrawing into that shy kid that I used to be at home, and in that instant, I knew I was in trouble.

At that point, the only tools I had available to me to overcome my withdrawn state were my martial arts practice and meditation. So, for weeks, after countless hours of physical and mental abuse in my basic training, I would spend my off-hours practicing my martial arts and my meditation, hoping that I would be able to push myself back into my confident state. But no matter how hard I tried, the tremendous amount of aggressive energy that I would feel at the entire base would just push me back into my withdrawn state, until I discovered the power of alcohol.

Unlike some other militaries around the world, the Dutch Navy allows alcohol to be served in mess halls and I discovered that next to having a talent for martial arts, I also had a talent for drinking. I discovered very early on that with every drink, I would feel even more powerful and confident, like I had while training in martial arts. And the more drunk I was, the more indestructible and outgoing I felt. After a while, I started to like myself a lot more when I was drinking than when I was sober. My drinking became a portal for me to go to a place where I would feel powerful, like my old warrior self, and I found myself slowly erasing my withdrawn persona by prolonging my drinking and shortening the time that I was sober.

For many years, I managed to get away with my drinking. I had become very good at masking my drinking from the authorities. I was so engaging and outgoing while I was drinking that people just thought I was charismatic by nature and never questioned my drinking. Somehow, I was able to perfectly balance my drinking with my work, and I never forfeited on my duties, until one night, I did.

One night, during one of my shifts, the inevitable happened. I showed up for work so drunk that I fell asleep at my post. While I was in my drunken stupor, my superior officer walked in and caught me drunk out of my mind. This prompted a flash inspection where my superior officer found more alcohol in my bedside locker than clothes, and that was the end of my sailing adventures.

One thing I will forever be grateful for was that the Dutch Royal Navy doesn't fire people for addiction, but instead place them in one of the Dutch Naval Bases and supports them by putting them through a mandatory rehabilitation program that includes intense physical and mental therapy. As a stroke of luck, the naval base that I was assigned to for my rehabilitation was a marine base on the Caribbean Island of Curacao. Curacao is still a Dutch Colony today and hence has a Dutch Marine base called Pareira Naval Base. Yes, I can hear what you are thinking. After getting caught being drunk on duty, he doesn't get shipped off to some hole in the Arctic, but instead gets shipped off to a beach paradise. Well, I never did say I wasn't lucky.

An interesting phenomenon about the Caribbean, and Curaçao in particular, is the positive energy the island exudes. Not a day goes by where the sun isn't shining. There is this constant sound of an ocean breeze combined with the ocean waves that is just magical. The people on the island are extremely warm, welcoming, and fun-loving. Mixed in with the ocean sounds, there is always Caribbean music playing and everywhere you look, someone is dancing. Even the energy at Pareira Naval base was always light and fun. From the first day that I set foot on Curaçao, I knew that I had arrived someplace magical. A place where I could heal.

Of course, being assigned to the Marines in the Caribbean in the late 1980s was not a total walk in the park. The late 80s was the height of the Columbian Drug Wars and the Caribbean was the body of water through which Pablo Escobar's armies of drug traffickers shipped their cocaine to the United States. The Dutch Navy and the Marines on Curacao were responsible for policing those waters between Curacao and Columbia, and I found myself being assigned to train and operate with the Marines as their communications and intelligence specialist.

And when not training, I had to attend meetings with a naval therapist, to support me in overcoming my addiction to alcohol.

Despite that fact that I found myself in paradise, starting my healing journey as an alcoholic while training with the Marines for six hours every day was no walk in the park. Saying that I was in rough shape after years of alcohol abuse is an understatement. I was like a walking corpse and the first few weeks of training were probably the toughest I had ever experienced. During those first few weeks, there was not a day that went by when I didn't think I was going to die. Luckily, I didn't die. And every day as I sobered up a little more, thanks to a combination of the training, my therapy, and being on this magical island, I could feel myself coming back to life.

It was during this period that I also became reintroduced to my love for martial arts. Located outside the naval base where I was stationed was a small old dilapidated schoolhouse that looked like it could have been a small church in its previous life. That small school was run by one of the humblest teachers I have ever met in my life. His name was Gobin Persaud and Master Gobin was a direct student of Master Oshima, who in return was a direct student of the father of modern karate, Master Gichin Funakoshi.

From his humble little karate school, Master Gobin was not only a teacher of Master Funakoshi's Karate, but also an Energy healer, and practitioner of traditional Chinese medicine. One night, after finishing my training with the Marines, I decided to go for a walk outside the barracks and stumbled upon this little school where practice was in full swing. I stood and watched from outside for a while, remembering my days as a martial artist. Seeing Master Gobin teach was like something I had never seen before. Even though he was getting on in age, his physical prowess was incredible. The grace at which he would move across the dojo floor as he was demonstrating techniques and forms to his students was awe inspiring. But what caught me offguard was his energy. As he was demonstrating the techniques, I could actually feel the Energy from his punches pass from his fists and travel through the walls of his school and hit me right in the chest.

True to Master Gobin's humble and inviting nature, he saw me standing outside that night and he immediately invited me in to sit with his students. Sitting with his students on the dojo floor observing Master Gobin teach his class, I began to reconnect with my former martial arts past. And at that moment, something inside me told me that I needed to become Master Gobin's student. From that night on, I spent almost every waking moment as a student of Master Gobin, where he not only taught me traditional Funakoshin Karate, but he also taught me how to master my own Ki, or energy through extreme physical and mental conditioning combined with advanced meditation and Energy projection practices. Some of these practices included maintaining painful stances for hours on end, twenty-four hour training sessions, and even breath-hold diving in the beautiful Caribbean waters around Curacao.

One could say that studying under Master Gobin was a critical turning point in my life and it was the beginning of my journey as a new and improved version of myself. I continued training under master Gobin for almost a year before being cleared to go back to sea duty. I left Master Gobin, my fellow karate students, and Curacao a changed man, and have never touched a drop of alcohol since. Sadly, Master Gobin passed away in 2014. Even though he is no longer with us, his teachings will stay with me forever.

After my deployment in Curacao, I returned home a completely changed person from when I left. I was much more confident and had developed an incredible level of awareness that I had never experienced before. On top of that, I was also in the best mental and physical shape of my life. I remember sitting in the military airplane on my way back to the Netherlands where I was to await orders for my next deployment. While sitting on this eight-hour flight, I was thinking about my one year transformation, and how I really liked who I had become in that one year. At that moment, a rush of sadness came over me as I imagined myself having to go back to living in the military environment where I had become an alcoholic prior to my transformation. The closer the airplane took me to home, the stronger the urge became that it was time for me to make a change in my life and my career. My transformation would not be complete unless I chose to retire from the military after ten years of service, so I could carve out a new life for myself. Even though I had no idea what I was going to do after leaving the military, my intuition strongly urged that it was time for me to make a change. And in that moment, I decided, it was time for me to move on to the next chapter of my life, even though I had no idea what that was going to be.

Chapter 2

Confessions of a Horrible Boss

Entering civilian life after my stint with the military, I found myself jobless and without a paycheck for the first time in my life. Even though I had no projected income in the immediate foreseeable future, I continued my training and meditation. One evening in my living room, I was practicing a martial arts technique I had learned in Curacao from Master Gobin. In this exercise, the goal is to hold a single stance for as long as possible, and to use the strength of the mind to push away any thoughts of pain and suffering. The stance that I was holding was called the horse-riding stance, and it looks a lot like someone is sitting on an invisible chair. The objective of this exercise is to hold the stance for so long that the body eventually gives up sending pain signals to the brain. Until that time, the body fights with the mind to convince the mind to give in and give up. It does so by sending massive amounts of pain signals to the brain and by making the body shake like it's throwing a tantrum. However, after a while, if the mind does not give in, the body settles into the stance, stops shaking and stops sending pain signals to the brain. Once the body resigns to the mind's will, the Energy pathways in the body open up, providing an intense flow of Energy that increases our awareness and intuition.

After my body calmed down and I was no longer distracted by the feelings of pain and discomfort, I asked my awareness to expand from my body and into my living room and to just keep me company for a while. And in that moment, my intuition spoke to me like a wise master who had seen the future. That night, it revealed two valuable lessons to me.

The first lesson was that I was going to be OK, irrespective of whether I would be able to find a job or not. The second lesson it revealed to me was that the reason why I was so perceptive in detecting energy was because I was meant to use it to help people. And in that instant as, my life's purpose started to reveal itself to me, I became a man on a mission to figure out how I could live a life helping people.

The next day, I hopped onto my bicycle, first thing in the morning, and I headed to the unemployment office to collect my first unemployment check. I remember sitting in the waiting room and saw a poster that was advertising a new initiative by the government where they would sponsor anyone with more than ten years of work experience to be able to take one year sabbatical to learn a new trade and be offered eighty per cent of their salary, as long as they stayed in the program for that year. Staring at that poster, I smiled. That's what my intuition was telling me the night before. I was going to be just fine. I jumped up, ran to the reception, and applied for the program on the spot. Within a few weeks I was fully enrolled. One of the contingencies of the program was that I had to attend monthly meetings with a career coach, who would keep me accountable during my transition. This was my first experience with a coach, and it was one that would again change my life.

During my sessions with my coach, we explored my interests and passions, and I got to tell her about my experience in the military, my martial arts training, and also my battles with depression and alcoholism. In one of those sessions, it dawned on me that the times when I was happiest was when I was physically active. She asked me whether or not a career in the fitness industry could be worth exploring. At that moment, I remembered my horse-riding stance session in my living room and how my intuition told me that my purpose was to help people. Being a fitness instructor would enable me to combine my passion for fitness with my purpose to help people. That idea sounded really appealing to me, so I jumped at the opportunity and enrolled in the first available nine-month fitness certification program.

After a few months, I had become a member of the local Gold's Gym in my neighbourhood so that I could do my own workouts and work on my own fitness while I was studying to become a fitness instructor. After speaking to the owner of the gym about my journey towards becoming a fitness instructor, he offered that I could work at his gym at minimum wage, which would give me an opportunity to practice what I was learning in my certification program. Here I was, at twenty-seven years of age, working at the local Gold's Gym, cleaning bathrooms, washing laundry, scrubbing floors, and doing all of that with the largest smile on my face. I had never made that little money in my life and I had never been happier at the same time.

I remember one cold winter's morning, cycling to the local Gold's Gym during peak hour traffic. I barely made enough money to pay the rent, so driving a car was out of the question. On that morning, I was cycling along a typical Dutch canal, riding on a cobblestone road along a row of cars, all stuck in a traffic jam. It was so cold that morning that I had icicles coming out of my nose that looked like stalactites. Looking to my left, I could see the drivers in their warm and comfortable cars, on their way to their regular day jobs. Looking closely, I could see that not one of them was smiling or laughing. In fact, there was no expression whatsoever. To me, it looked as if each of those drivers was simply existing, but not truly living. I began to remember how I would drive to my work place each day while in the military, and I imagined that I must have looked exactly the same as those drivers that morning. Freezing on my bike, with stalactites coming out of my nose, I suddenly began to smile, because for the first time in my life, I came to a realization that doing a job where I was happy was the universe's way of telling me that I was on the right path. And that's when it hit me. Maybe, in my case, my depression was not just an illness per se, but more of a marker, like a stake in the ground, that would tell me that I am following the wrong path. In contrast, the happiness that I feel when doing something I love is another marker that I am moving in the right path. All of a sudden, it became clear to me that the universe's way of guiding me on my journey through this life is through my feelings and through my intuition. If it feels right, I'm happy. If it feels wrong, I become depressed. Eureka!

So, you'd think that with this kind of realization, I would have life figured out, right? Wrong! There was another important lesson for me to learn that would take me another fifteen years to realize. This I learned by becoming a horrible boss myself.

Shortly after becoming a certified fitness instructor, my new sense of direction sparked a passion for scientific knowledge within me. I discovered that the more I learned about exercise physiology, nutrition, and psychology, the more effective I became in helping people live more fulfilling lives. I found myself reading everything I could on any scientific topic that could help me become more knowledgeable and effective as a coach. After years of studying and working as a personal trainer, I had achieved a level of knowledge where I developed a reputation as being the smartest guy in the gym. No matter the size of the gym, I rarely met people with my level of expertise, and that gave me a feeling of confidence that I had become an expert in my field. And I loved being the expert in the room a little too much. I fell in love with the status of being an expert, and after a while, I started to place more value on my image as an expert than on the good that I was doing for people. Interestingly, as I'm thinking back on my life's journey, I realize that the more I pursued scientific knowledge to feed my ego rather than help people, the further I moved myself away from my sense of intuition. I became so determined to study and learn about my field that I gradually started to deprioritize the energy practices that I had learned from Master Gobin years before. And eventually, those practices became distant memories.

Fast forward twelve years. I moved to Singapore as one of the first fitness leaders in an emerging industry. I completed a degree in Health Sciences and became an international fitness educator. One could say that I was flying high in my career and life was good. But I wanted more. In my role as an international educator, I had the privilege of visiting many large scale gyms in the region, and began to develop a desire to build my own club. I felt confident that with my high levels of expertise, operating my own club would be a natural next step for me. With zero experience of running a business, I had become arrogant enough to believe that I knew everything there was to know about building my own company.

Unsurprisingly, with my reputation in the industry, finding fellow investors was quite easy, and I found three partners who either had no fitness industry experience, or had very little experience. Unfortunately, they also did not have experience in running a business. That was fine by me though since I considered myself the expert in the partnership. So, with my knowledge and experience, we were set up for success, or so I foolishly thought. In 2007, we opened SPEED Institute, South East Asia's first and largest athlete development centre, and it was awesome. It was a beautiful facility that catered to both children and adults. It had indoor sprinting lanes, a reaction wall, and the most cutting-edge strength equipment that money could buy. We ran athlete development classes for adults in the mornings and evening, while booking out the facility to kids in after-school programs. Using my operational and scientific knowledge, I single-handedly developed a concept for group training classes that combined sports training exercises and mental strength training techniques at the same time. With that concept in mind, I designed all the class programs and athlete development curriculums, hired, and trained the staff-trainers, and over-saw the coaching standards. By the time I was done, I had created a training facility that rivalled even the best professional athlete training facilities in the United States. My concept was a big hit with the public and business was going well. My operational success further fuelled my delusion that I was amazing at my job, and that's when things started to go wrong.

While I was so engaged in the day-to-day operations of the business, two of my business partners tried their best to support me by running the business administration and marketing; but with their limited experience, they soon found themselves out of their depth. Despite their lack of experience, they worked tirelessly to keep the company running, but because I was so focused on the short-term operations of the gym, I never thought about appreciating their challenges. I would arrive in the morning at six o'clock to start the coaching, and one of them would already be in the office. At ten o'clock, after the last night class, I would leave, and they would still be in the office. Not once did I ever acknowledge their commitment and sacrifice. In hindsight, I believe that I was so determined to create a fantastic experience for my students that I lost sight of the well-being of my partners.

On the training floor, I wasn't any better as a leader to my team either. My success as a coach was validation to me that I was the expert in my gym. I was so firmly vested in my knowledge that I would not accept input or recommendations from the other coaches. In fact, I had become so fixed in my views that I would see feedback as criticism and would respond to any feedback from my team with hostility. Over time, my trainers stopped trying to give creative input and instead, simply complied with what I wanted as I was the boss. The lack of input from my team that I had created only further fuelled my delusion that I was good at what I.

After about six months of operations, things started to go south. I remember, during one of our monthly shareholders' meetings, my two partners tried to give me feedback on how they felt I was running the training floor with an iron fist and asked if I could also get more involved in the other aspects of the business to help them out. At that moment, I came to the realization that I had no respect for these two partners, and I felt that they did not respect me. I mean, how could they be so arrogant to dare to suggest that I, the super trainer, was doing less than an incredible job? Who were they to criticize my brilliance? Did they not see the amount of work, energy, and devotion I was putting into this company? I felt an unspeakable rage come over me. But, instead of acting out in anger, I did the opposite. I shut down, stopped communicating with my partners, and just focused on my work on the training floor.

Over time, the atmosphere at work had become so toxic, it was unbearable. My trainers stopped showing up for work and I found myself taking on even more work, which further fuelled my resentment. After a while, it felt like I was running the operations all by myself and I was not getting any support. I began to see myself as a victim and blamed everybody else for the horrible situation I was in. Slowly but surely, as my fatigue levels, stress, and resentment rose to a critical level, I once again started to experience episodes of depression, something I thought I had left behind me forever.

Things became so bad that I could not set foot into my own company without crying uncontrollably. I remember standing in front of the doors of my own gym, looking at the large SPEED Institute sign hanging over the door, and tears running down my face. It was as if the doors had become an impenetrable barrier. My feet became heavy, like they were set in cement, and no matter how hard I tried, I just could not get myself through the doors. At that moment, I realized that I could not carry on anymore. I turned around, went home, and wrote my partners an email that I was resigning from my own company.

We all met shortly after and we agreed that I would stay on as a silent partner, but would recuse myself from any business decisions, moving forward. After leaving that meeting, I never set foot in my own company ever again. Yet, that wasn't the end of the lesson.

After my departure, the remaining partners hired a chief operating officer to take over my duties, and to my surprise, he did an incredible job. He actually did a much better job than I did, and that was humbling. Together with my partners, he turned the business around and once again made SPEED Institute a profitable business that flourished. Upon seeing the success of the company without me, I slowly came to the realization that even though my motives were noble, I had become my own company's enemy. In my single-minded determination, I became the saboteur of my own success and that realization was not easy for me. A few years later, one of my partners offered to buy the business from the remaining partners and that was the end of my experience with SPEED Institute and my experience as a horrible boss. For me, as traumatic as the experience was, it was a very important lesson on ego. This experience was a valuable lesson that taught me how ego can devastate our abilities to achieve success. And with that realization, I decided I needed to make a change.

My ego, and the subsequent mismanagement of my own company, not only hurt me, but it also hurt my partners and my staff. First, they had to deal with me every single day that I was present while working at SPEED, and then they had to work even harder to pick up the pieces after I had left. The realization that I had let them down left me with a sense of shame, but it also triggered a sense of fascination for leadership. With that realization and with a desire to make a change, I decided to go back to school where I pursued a master's degree in Neuroscience of Leadership, which became the start of my journey as an executive leadership coach. Even today, many years later, I still refer back to the many mistakes I made as a business leader in my coaching practice. I still believe to this day that if I hadn't had the insight that I was a horrible boss, I wouldn't be as effective as I am today as an executive leadership coach. It was that moment of realization that sparked a whole new path for me into becoming who I am today.

Even so, getting to where I am today was not easy. Learning to see the amazing gifts that my depression, my natural intuition, my ego, and subsequent failures gave me took me a long time. For the longest time, even when I was studying in the master's program, I would have this voice at the back of my head, telling me that I was not worthy of being successful. I had this image in my mind, like an ever-repeating story, that because I had failed so many times in life, I would have nothing of value to offer to executives and leaders. And while I was studying to be a coach, I really struggled with that. I often asked myself whether or not I should just drop out, give up, and go back to what I knew best, which was being a personal trainer. Yet, even though I had these thoughts rolling around in my head, my intuition kept telling me that I needed to stay on the course and finish my education. This conflict stayed with me for a while, but thankfully, I let my intuition lead me down this new path, and soon, it would present me with an incredible opportunity to see myself as being someone who does have a lot of value to offer this world.

That pivotal lesson came while I was still enrolled in the master's program. I was invited by the Center for Creative Leadership to visit their campus in Colorado Springs and to observe one of their five-day leadership development programs. I remember being really surprised that one of the most prestigious leadership development organizations in the world would invite me for a visit, but that they were actually interested in the Neuroscience of Leadership research that I was doing for my thesis.

I still remember that day like it was yesterday. It was late January on a Monday morning. As I stepped out of the taxi and looked at the massive campus, I was awestricken. The architecture of this complex was designed to inspire wonder, while simultaneously blending in perfectly with the local architecture of mountain living. Behind the complex, as if it was rising from the roof of this complex, was the magnificent Pike's Peak; behind that was the bluest sky I had ever seen. I remember just standing there and feeling a little out of my comfort zone. As I was standing there with my mouth open, I noticed the people who were walking around me, getting ready to go to work or be in one of the many leadership classes.

I saw one four-star army general and two admirals, as well as a number of extremely well-dressed leaders who looked like they were way out of my league. And what's even funnier is that I was standing there in a suit that I had borrowed from a friend of mine who warned me that I was going to need a good suit.

I gathered up my courage, took a deep breath, pulled up the slightly baggy pants, and headed for the door. Once inside, however, I noticed that everyone was extremely down to earth and behaving in a very casual manner. The admirals and the generals were mingling with plain-clothed people and they were all just very casual and relaxed in their demeanour. The leadership team running the program welcomed me with open arms and were even asking me for feedback on everything, showing genuine interest in whatever observations I could share. Honestly, there wasn't a lot I could share because that place was polished to a tee.

The program I got to observe was one of their flagship leadership programs that fully dissects the habits and behaviours of very senior leaders in both the military and Fortune 500 companies. These leaders had to undergo a series of psychometric tests and 360-degree feedback assessments prior to their program and they, then, spent the five days dissecting themselves.

For the first few days, I couldn't help but sit there at the back of the class and wonder how I was ever going to be able to be a good coach for such accomplished leaders. I mean, these were the most successful and accomplished leaders in the United States, and possibly the world, and I couldn't help but feel a little bit inferior, especially each time I had to pull my borrowed pants up.

However, that all started to change when the leaders were presenting the outcomes of their assessments to the group. What I learned at that moment was that each of those leaders, no matter how polished and accomplished they looked, were just human beings like me. The feedback that they received from their respective teams, their fellow leader-students, and from the faculty was exactly the same type of stuff that I had been ashamed of in myself. There was one leader who received very negative feedback for being too aggressive in his demeanour, another one was perceived as being too passive, a third was perceived as being a poor communicator and so on. As the week went on, I started to see a very human and vulnerable side to each of those incredibly accomplished leaders; they all came to the realization that at sometime or the other, each and every one of them were perceived as being horrible bosses. As we got to the final days of the program, the big step for each of the leaders was to not just acknowledge in what areas they needed to improve, but to also learn to accept that they had been presented with the gift of insight into themselves.

I remember walking away from that campus at the end of the week—after the program had been completed—being extremely moved, humbled, and inspired. It was at that moment that I realized that my failures and shortcomings were not failures and shortcomings. In fact, they were simply indicators or markers that function like guides toward where I needed to go in my life. And just like those leaders in the leadership program, we all need to experience these experiences to become who we need to be. I realized that day that I was just as human as they were and that we all struggle with making the most out of our experiences in life. It was then and there that I learned that I deserved to be the best coach that I could be; not despite my failures and shortcomings, but because of them.

What I learned from this is that at some point in your career, you too were perceived by the people you work with as a horrible boss; no matter how good your intentions are, how passionate you are, or how hard you try to be a good boss. Someone out there, at some point in time, is going to think of you as a horrible boss. What I would like to ask you is, 'At what point in your day, week, month, year, or career, do you remember possibly being a horrible boss? How long ago was it that you recognized that you were a horrible boss and what did you learn about yourself in the process?'

Now, thinking forward, I would also like you to think about how many missed opportunities you may have had where you were not aware that you were being a horrible boss, just like me. What was missing in your relationship with yourself, with your team-members, your superiors, or your subordinates, that prevented you from receiving this incredible gift for growth?

Now that we have established that we have all been horrible bosses at some point in our lives, let's take a look at the impact a boss has on the organizational climate and on the company's bottom line.

Chapter 3

A Boss Creates the Weather

A few years ago, I received a call from an angel investor who was looking to invest in a large gym chain in Indonesia as part of their heavily diversified portfolio. They had their eyes set on a particular global wellness and lifestyle brand, and were looking into acquiring the franchise for one of the Southeast Asian countries. Their request was to meet up for coffee and pick my brain on whether or not this would be a good investment for them. I took a moment to deliberate on this, since this was a request that does not happen every day. As an executive coach, my work is more related to helping leaders take a deeper dive into the effectiveness of their leadership and to partner with them in honing their skills where needed. Of course, I did understand why this investor would want to speak to me since I had over twenty years of experience working in the wellness industry; so I decided to meet with him and to have a chat about their experience so far.

A few days later, we met at a local Starbucks in Singapore where I was enthusiastically greeted by one of the managing directors of the investment company. After ordering coffee, he began to fill me in on the situation regarding the gym franchise. He mentioned that as a gym chain, the global fitness brand is one of the oldest and largest fitness organizations in the world and is headquartered in the United States. The reason why this investor was interested in speaking to me was because he was approached by the current franchise owner in Southeast Asia who at that point owned twenty large gyms in Southeast Asia and was looking for additional funding to expand the brand. Of course, these types of investments are not uncommon in large companies, so I asked him a fundamental coaching question, 'What are you, as the investor, hoping to accomplish from the acquisition, and on a scale of one to ten, how confident are you that this decision will produce the results you desire?' The moment I asked him that question, he looked me deep in the eyes and said, 'You know, I've been doing this for a very long time and usually, I have a very good nose for these types of opportunities. On paper, everything looks incredibly promising. The numbers look good and the market research shows great opportunity for exponential growth. However, I have no experience in the fitness industry and something is telling me that I should seek council from an expert who knows the industry and the operations before making this investment.'

By the end of our conversation, he invited me to fly to Thailand and to do one last due diligence check to dot the i's before making the investment. Within one week, I found myself in Bangkok, where I was staying at the heart of the city at the Hyatt Regency. My objective was to visit all twenty clubs of this fitness chain as well as the gym chain's local headquarters, and to interview the current CEO of the company and all line- and gym-managers to get a feel of the operations, and the current culture of the organization.

The very next day, I was picked up early in the morning by the CEO's driver and transported in their luxury minivan to start my observations at the local HQ. Now, commuting in Bangkok is in itself quite an adventure. Traffic is so chaotic that it takes approximately two hours to get somewhere that would normally take ten minutes without traffic. This is not an exaggeration. What this meant was that even though my meeting was at 8 a.m., the driver had to collect me at 6.30 a.m. to make sure that I made it on time. After exactly 90 minutes of enjoying the luxury van, I made it to the HQ in time for my meeting with the CEO and his leadership team. The CEO's office building was impressively designed, as if it were making the statement, 'Here is the epitome of status, luxury, and excellence.' In typical high status fashion, the company had a doorman who graciously let me in to the office. Once inside, the ground floor of the office was designed as a long rectangle with the offices of the senior leaders all along both sides and cubicles for support staff in the middle.

I have had the privilege of doing many culture surveys in my career as a coach. One technique that I still find most effective is to walk into an office building and just allow myself to absorb the Energy of the office. I have given myself three different categories for describing an office culture in the form of the weather. So, as I started walking through the office and cubicle area, I imagined what type of weather this office felt like. Whenever I do this in a new company, I give myself one of three choices. Is the weather that I feel rainy and miserable? Is it overcast and gloomy? Or is it a bright and sunny day in the office? Well, in this case, I couldn't help but feel the weather as being overcast and gloomy at best.

As I walked through the facility, I noticed how everyone was frantically working on something. They all had their heads down in their cubicles and the place was eerily quiet for an office its size. I couldn't help but wonder if everyone was actually busy working or whether they were all just keeping their heads down so as to avoid unwanted attention from anyone.

At the back of the building was the entrance to the CEO's office. It was locked. No, the door wasn't just closed, the door was actually locked from the inside. Outside the CEO's office was the cubicle of the CEO's personal assistant. She informed me that the CEO was running a little late, but he would be with me shortly. I decided to walk around the office and poke my head into the doors of the offices that were all lined up on the outsides of the bullpen to introduce myself to the leaders individually. After a few minutes, the personal assistant came to get me and told me that the CEO was ready to see me.

Entering the CEO's office, it was like stepping onto the set of the TV show *Suits*. The CEO's corner office looked just like that of Harvey Specter's office, including sports memorabilia and a large oakwood desk. The only difference was this CEO's office also included a twelve-person conference table.

Sitting behind his desk, typing busily on his computer, the CEO didn't look up, but waved me into the office while looking down at his laptop screen and pointed me towards the general direction of the conference table. I sat down politely and continued to admire his office, while he was finishing up what he was doing. As I took a moment to take in my new environment, I couldn't help but notice that his window-side wall was full of superhero collectibles from the Marvel universe, including a life-size Iron Man suit that was displayed in a wall-to-ceiling glass cabinet. The cabinet looked like it was custom built for that specific Iron Man Suit. Honestly, I felt like I had stepped out of reality and into some fantasy office on a movie set.

Once he finished doing what he was doing, he greeted me more formally by shaking my hand and sat across from me on the other side of the massive boardroom table. After a bit of small talk, he summoned his assistant to call in the rest of the leadership team so that we could start with the briefing. His mannerism in how he summoned his assistant was extremely authoritarian. He did not use words such as 'please' and 'thank you', and his tone of voice was very demanding. Whether it was conscious or not on his part, the impression that I got was that he was trying to project a sense of authority.

Another observation that I couldn't help but make was that the CEO looked to be quite out of shape. He had a large belly, poor posture, and he looked extremely tired, as if he was trying to portray that all he did in life was work. The reason why I found this fascinating was because the company I was assessing was a fitness company, and at first glance, it did not look to me as if the leader of the company was a man who embodied his brand. I decided to take a mental note of all my observations so far, but didn't want to draw any conclusions until I had done a thorough analysis.

Shortly after sending his personal assistant to summon the team, the rest of the leadership team came into the office and joined us around the conference table. The energy of each member of the team was subdued and flat. There was no joking around, laughter, or fun. I tried to break the ice by cracking a few lighthearted jokes, but the jokes were met with very subdued smiles and that was that. It seemed to me like the team had long figured out that this CEO's office was a place where serious business was done and fun was surely not on the menu.

In that first meeting, the CEO gave a lengthy PowerPoint presentation where he did a deep dive into the financial and operational status of the company. After he was done, the other leaders also gave short presentations on things they were working on, such as customer service, member experience, membership attrition rates, personal training, group fitness programs, and so on.

Once everyone had done their presentations, I explained that I would be looking into the company culture and asked them what they felt the company culture was. That question was met with a lot of shifting in their chairs and everyone was reluctant to give their input, until the CEO spoke. What he told me was very interesting. He mentioned to me that good people are really hard to find and he always found himself surrounded by incompetent people, which infuriated him. He said that if only he could get good people onboard, his business would do extremely well, and the company culture would not be an issue. In other words, he felt like his company's culture was a culture of incompetence, and that he was the only competent person there.

I spent the next week visiting all twenty of the clubs, observing their operations, and interviewing their staff. Unsurprisingly, my observations of the club operations reflected the cultural weather at the headquarters. Staff members all tried to look busy and there was absolutely no laughter in these clubs. At a place where people were supposed to be inspiring and doing something they loved, the atmosphere of every single club was gloomy at best. One surprising similarity that I noticed in every club was the type of conversation I would have with the numerous managers. After sitting down with each manager, I would ask them a simple question, 'How are you doing?' The answer by each manager was exactly the same. Their default answer would be to tell me about how much revenue the club was generating from membership sales and personal training. They would then go on to tell me about their marketing and sales strategies to try to boost sales. After taking time to listen to their default answer, I would repeat the question again, 'How are *you* doing?' which would just be met with puzzled looks. What I began to realize was that the managers never learned how to have a conversation about what they thought or what they felt. The only conversations that were initiated from the CEO's office was that of numbers.

In our conversations, I would give them a series of ten statements that reflect the type of culture and ask them to score each statement with a score from one to ten, one being the lowest and ten being the highest scores. Using the Net Promoter Scoring system—which is a way of scoring one's satisfaction with a company or a service—a culture score below six would reflect very poor weather, a score between six and eight would be considered gloomy weather, and a score of eight and above would be sunny weather. The ten statements I gave were:

1. I tell others great things about my company.
2. I would recommend my company to my family and friends.
3. I feel strongly connected to this company and the brand.
4. This company encourages new ideas and innovation.
5. If asked, I could clearly explain my company's vision.
6. Working here gives me a sense of accomplishment.
7. My job description is extremely clear to me.
8. My superiors provide me with the support I need to be successful.
9. My superiors care about me and my well-being.
10. My future career opportunities look good at this company.

Once I was done with the interviews, I quantified the scores from the questionnaires. It showed an average score of six out of ten, which would present the organizational weather as being 'Gloomy'. Interestingly, the scores of this short questionnaire quite accurately reflected the gloomy weather I was feeling at the head office too. Clearly, the weather from the headquarters had spilled over to all of the clubs and it was inhibiting the quality of operations, customer service, and sales of all the clubs and thus having a detrimental effect on the revenue of the entire organization.

After my one week of observations, I wrote a detailed analysis of my findings. In my report, I recommended two critical actions which if ignored would greatly inhibit company growth. The first recommendation was to initiate a culture change strategy. The second was to either have the current CEO undergo intense coaching or to have him removed from his position and be replaced by a CEO who could create a stronger culture.

Upon my suggestion, the investor set a condition that a vigorous culture shift initiative needed to be implemented. However, because the CEO was also an investor in the company, the investor decided against suggesting coaching or replacing the current CEO. The investor then requested me if I could develop the culture change strategy. I spent the next three months setting in place a strategy that would include all members of the organization, including the CEO. Interestingly, the entire organization responded enthusiastically to the new changes, except for one person. You got it, the CEO. Week by week, the CEO could see subtle changes in the behaviour of his people, and as their effectiveness improved, the CEO's enthusiasm decreased. Over time, his collaboration efforts gradually diminished from being cooperative, to being resigned, to becoming resentful. After about three months, he had grown so resentful that he started sabotaging any culture initiatives. For example, he would deny any budget for the initiative. He would not permit people to attend training sessions during work hours, and he created an inner circle of his closest allies in the company. Using that inner circle, he used them to spread rumours and make threats that he would fire anybody who would challenge his authority. Using his inner circle, he was able to obstruct any progress of the changed management program. Finally, the investor contacted me and said that the CEO had decided to discontinue the culture change initiative and that they were going to try to make the business profitable without the culture initiative. They thanked me for my service, and I headed back home.

One year later, I remember bumping into one of the company's leadership team members while travelling and I asked him how things were going. He shook his head and said that sadly the company was on the brink of going bankrupt and there was no solution anywhere in sight. The CEO was still locking himself in his office and the weather in the organization had worsened to being miserable, despite a large injection of cash from the investor.

Personally, I found this quite unfortunate as I had come to love the one thousand staff members who were all trying so hard to make things work for the company. Sadly, the CEO, who was also the founder of the company, had grown into being the company's worst enemy by resisting any input or assistance from anyone in the company.

It reminded me a lot of the saboteur that I once was when I had founded my own gym. Just as my ego had gotten in the way of my company's success, so too had the ego of this CEO.

What I learned from this experience was that the weather in any company is directly linked to the weather that is projected by the leader of the organization. Initiating a culture-change strategy without cooperation from the most senior leader is destined to fail, and without the leader's support, the culture weather is likely not going to improve.

So, based on this story, a few questions that I would ask you to think about are:

1. What type of weather do you want in your organization, your team, or even in your relationships with your loved ones?

2. In your opinion, how's the weather currently? Based on the ten questions in the previous questionnaire, what would your score be?

3. What are you doing as a boss, manager, partner, or even family member to contribute to the weather in your organization, team, or family?

4. How do the people in your organization, team, or family score the organization, team, or family?

5. Finally, if any of the above scores are below ten, what would you need to do differently in your daily routine to facilitate achieving a higher score?

Knowing the answers to these questions, you are going to be able to draw a clear picture of your involvement in the weather of your company, team, or family. With this knowledge, you will then be able to make a conscious decision about the role you want to play in the overall climate of the organization and what will be required of you to influence the climate in your organization, team, or family.

Chapter 4

Three Pillars of Wisdom

One of the privileges of my work is that I get paid to have incredibly stimulating conversations with amazing people. On some days, conversations with leaders could be in the subject area of business strategy, on other days, it could be on matters relating to leadership, or communication skills, and so on. However, every now and then, coaching conversations with leaders can take a very personal and philosophical turn.

One of the reasons for this is that being a senior leader in an organization can feel extremely isolating sometimes. In fact, a lot of research has been conducted on loneliness in leadership since the mid-1980s, showing that more than 50 per cent of leaders tend to feel lonely in their positions, which can be a tremendous physical and psychological burden on leaders' performance and health. Having some form of emotional support system within the organization, such as support groups or confidants to talk to, can be difficult since many leaders feel that they need to present themselves in a manner that exudes confidence and substance so that they can continue to inspire confidence in their people. A popular term for this is leadership presence.

Many times, I am brought into organizations to serve as an independent and objective partner with whom the leader can feel a deeper emotional connection and support, a method which has been shown to be extremely effective in lessening the side-effects of loneliness in leaders. A common conversation that arises regularly with such leaders is about the challenges they face in trying to manage their own emotions while exhibiting a certain presence as a leader that inspires confidence in their people. What I find interesting is that Leadership Presence still seems to be misunderstood by many leaders and even leadership consultants.

Oftentimes, when asking leaders what their understanding of Leadership Presence is, they share that their definition of Leadership Presence is about displaying themselves in a certain way that they think will inspire, motivate, and give confidence to the people they work with. The common misconception that often arises from this is that they must put on a front that allows them to showcase themselves in a way that projects confidence and substance at all times. The challenge of this is that leaders are only human, and with being human comes the reality that, at times, we aren't confident and that we can be as vulnerable as any other human being in the organization.

Putting up a 'front' that they think inspires confidence in their people may come at a very high cost. Firstly, many leaders who believe they need to present themselves in a particular way run the risk of feeling inauthentic. Secondly, pretending to be something that we are not can be utterly exhausting.

Recently, I was running a program called 'Learning with Leaders'. Part leadership training and part loneliness support group, 'Learning with Leaders' gives leaders of organizations an opportunity to share their perspectives on leadership and management practices with other leaders from different organizations. This support group provides them with a safe place where they can be themselves, share different perspectives about life and leadership, and where they can be vulnerable.

In one of our sessions, the topic of Leadership Presence came up and we had an extremely insightful conversation about what Leadership Presence was to them. In just a few minutes, every person pretty much agreed that projecting themselves in a way that inspires confidence in their people is one of the most important factors of Leadership Presence. However, the conversation became very interesting when I asked, 'What is it that we need to project to inspire confidence in others?' I pulled out my whiteboard and asked the class to create a list of characteristics and behaviours that they felt would inspire confidence in their people.

The class came up with quite a list, ranging from being confident, being authentic, being in control, being honest, being decisive, to being knowledgeable, being trustworthy, being empathetic, being balanced, and so on. Once we exhausted all the characteristics, I asked the class to take a moment to just absorb all of the characteristics and reflect on how they would rank these characteristics from most important to least important. This question sparked a fantastic conversation around what each leader values in Leadership Presence. Eventually, the team decided to vote on each point. Their consensus was that even though each characteristic weighed heavily, being knowledgeable ranked in their eyes as the most important factor. When asked why this characteristic would weigh heavier than something like being honest or trustworthy, they replied that in business, a leader who knows the business and industry in and out would likely project a lot of confidence and with that inspire confidence in others.

As the class was starting to feel good about their reasoning around being knowledgeable, I asked the class, 'What if there's something else? What if there's a different way of being that allows us to embody not just being knowledgeable, but includes all of the characteristics that you've listed, and more?' That question caught their attention.

I then went on to tell a story about one of my karate teacher's from when I was a teenager. Back in my younger years, I was heavily inspired by my martial arts movie heroes like Bruce Lee, Chuck Norris, and Jean-Claude Van Damme. As a youngster, I learned that I had a talent for combat. I was quick, had fast reflexes, stamina and power, and an intuition that helped me anticipate the opponent's moves before they executed it. Thanks to these talents that I was born with, I quickly rose through the national ranks in competition until I hit a competition plateau. I remember breezing through the regional and provincial championships as a fighter, but as I entered the national championship levels, things changed. The other fighters were at least just as quick, just as skilled, and often had better reflexes than me. No matter how hard I trained while preparing for tournaments, I would be stopped short in the opening rounds of the tournament, resulting in an early departure.

Over time, this constant losing really started to play on my confidence. I began to doubt my abilities as a fighter, and even found myself waking up on some days, wondering if martial arts was really something I wanted to continue pursuing. My confidence dropped so much that even during practice in my local school, where I was considered one of the best fighters, I would lose against the most elementary fighters. I had officially fallen into my first slump. Just walking onto the mat, a place that had once given me such great joy, was now becoming something I would dread. I remember, one day during practice, all of the students were in a kneeling position around the tatami mat as the teacher would call up students to pair off against each other in kumite. For the first time in my life, I remember looking down, hoping that my teacher would not call my name. Of course, as if he could sense it, he called me up onto the mat to fight another one of his students who was much lower ranked than me. I remember standing up from my kneeling position and my body feeling heavy. A body that was used to moving with the speed and grace of a cat felt like it was moving like a hippo. Not that I have anything against hippos, but it felt like my body was not mine, and that I had been teleported into a completely different body.

As you can imagine, it didn't take long for me to get my buttocks handed to me by a student who was many years my junior. Humiliated and frustrated, I bowed my head in disgrace and started to cry in front of the class. I looked up at my teacher who looked back and just waited. I said to him, 'I don't understand; why am I so bad at this?' 'Bad at what?' asked my teacher. 'At everything,' I answered. He looked at me deeply and said, 'I think you're only bad at one thing. Losing!' I looked at him, totally puzzled, and he said, 'Son, one thing I have learned from my life as a martial artist is that if you really want to win at anything, you must first learn how to lose.' At that moment, it was as if my teacher had taken a brick and smashed some sense in me. It was that one sentence that opened my eyes to a whole new world. Learning how to lose is not a slump or a rut. It's a critical component of development, and without losing, there can't be winning.

At that moment, my teacher shared a piece of wisdom that he had learned through his experience and not from any martial arts handbook.

And that one piece of insightful wisdom he shared with me reshaped my personal relationship with losing. I pulled myself together on the mat and asked my teacher and sparring partner if we could go again. My teacher smiled and agreed. I felt a shift in my body and it began to feel lighter as I looked differently at the idea of losing. Embracing losing as a step towards winning, I found myself again, and walked off the mat no longer a victim of my losses, but a victor of my learnings.

After telling my leadership class this story, I asked the group what it was that I really needed in my teacher that day. Was it his incredible knowledge and skill in martial arts, or was it his wisdom? Everyone unanimously agreed that wisdom trumps knowledge in leadership.

I went on to share with them a quote that I learned from one of the wisest people I know, my daughter, Kilani. Ever since she was born, she has had this incredible sense about her that just blows me away and I have learned much from her wisdom in my life. When Kilani was growing up, my wife and I always prioritized gaining valuable life experiences such as travelling around the world, meeting interesting people, and learning things they don't teach in schools, to help her gain perspectives that had, hopefully, shaped her into the amazing adult that she is today.

Now that Kilani's an adult, we get to have some really deep, philosophical, and insightful conversations together. Just recently, she and I were having a conversation about wisdom. Thinking back on her childhood, Kilani said to me, 'You know, one thing I learned, growing up with you guys, is that we gain knowledge through studying, we gain learning through practice, but wisdom, we gain through living. And I'm really grateful that I had the opportunity to practice all three of those while growing up.'

I went on to explain to the class how the concept of wisdom in leadership really fascinates me. Scholars, philosophers, and religions have been writing about wisdom for millennia; yet, a clear definition of what wisdom really is still eludes us. It's a term that is widely accepted in our language. We all seem to have a basic understanding of what wisdom is and can recognize it when we see it, but most of us can't think of a clear definition. I put this to the test with my class of leaders and asked them to come up with their own definitions. Even though everyone felt they had a pretty good understanding of what it means to be wise, every member of the class had their own specific definition of what wisdom is.

I then went on to share with the group a research study conducted by researchers from the University of California, San Diego in 2013. In this research paper published by the *American Journal of Geriatric Psychiatry*, the researchers reviewed the empirical research on the topic of wisdom since the 1980s, so they could create a better understanding of the overlapping definitions, properties, and sub-components of wisdom. Interestingly, they identified nine common subcomponents of wisdom: (1) social decision making and pragmatic knowledge of life, such as social reasoning and life-skills, (2) prosocial attitudes, which include empathy, compassion, altruism, warmth, and a sense of fairness, (3) self-reflection and self-understanding, which relate to introspection, self-awareness, insight, and intuition, (4) acknowledgement of and coping effectively with uncertainty, (5) emotional homeostasis, which relates to affect regulation and self-control, (6) tolerance, which relates to being non-judgemental and accepting of other perspectives, (7) openness to new experiences, (8) spirituality, and (9) having a sense of humour.

I then asked the group, 'If a wise leader embodied these nine components of wisdom, would they be successful in inspiring, motivating, and instilling confidence in their people?' The group unanimously agreed. I then went on to discuss what is required of us to be able to access our wisdom. I told to the group something I have learned in my years of studying western science as a neuroscientist, Asian Philosophy, and martial arts. Each one of us on this planet has access to infinite amounts of wisdom, provided we apply all three pillars of wisdom. These three pillars, when applied together, give us deep-rooted insights and answers to even the most complex riddles and challenges that life can throw our way. The interesting thing about these three pillars is that many of us learn throughout our lives to rely on and trust only one or two of those pillars. In my opinion, this is what sets great and visionary leaders apart from average leaders and also horrible bosses.

These three pillars are:

1. The Knowing Pillar: Facts, information, skills, and rationality that have been acquired through experience, studying or learning.
2. The Feeling Pillar: Awareness of empathy, emotions, and moods in ourselves and others.
3. The Super-Sensing Pillar: Tapping into our intuition and to be consciously synchronized with the energy from our external and internal environments.

After explaining this to the class, I asked the members, 'Which of these three is most valued by most companies and managers in today's business climate?' Unanimously, the group agreed that most organizations are run using the Knowing Pillar. The reason for this is that most companies want to be able to quantify their growth and success. Making success tangible requires quantifying all processes into measurable data. This data then gives us an indication of what is working and what is not. Managers in organizations might look at that data and use their gut combined with their knowledge to take decisions on what steps need to be undertaken to ensure continued growth. Finally, some leaders might, then, use their ability to sense whether a particular strategy is working or not.

Unfortunately, and as proven by neuroscience, when relying too heavily on the Knowing Pillar, we tend to see only that which we pay attention to and discard all other information in the periphery as irrelevant. If I am running a department and all I pay attention to is the sales numbers of the team, I could fool myself into thinking that the team is successful when I see the sales numbers increase. Yet, there may be a lot going on around me that I am not seeing, simply because I'm not paying attention to them. For example, what is the culture of my team? What are they not telling me about how happy or unhappy they are? How adaptable are they to change? Our ability to feel and sense things helps us cast a wider net around us to help us develop some visibility around what we might not be seeing, which is crucial in the sustainability of any business. A great example of this is the fall of Nokia, where the CEO, Stephen Elop's final speech ended with, 'We didn't do anything wrong, but somehow, we lost.' Nokia is a great example of an organization that was once at the forefront of innovation using all three pillars in their growth. However, over time, as the organization grew into the largest mobile phone company in the world, they became obsessed with operating in the knowing space, and became increasingly operationally driven. Relying too heavily on operating in the knowing space, they lost their capacity for adaptability, and with the invention of the smartphone, Nokia became a dinosaur overnight.

In my opinion, one of the wisest questions leaders can ask themselves is, 'What am I not seeing here?' rather than saying, 'I know what is going on!' The truth is, as a leader, you do not know what is happening to your people, in your team, or even in your organization. You might like to think you do, but all you know is that which you are paying attention to. Relying too heavily on the knowing pillar, without applying the other two, might also put you at risk of suffering the same fate as Nokia.

Conversely, there are a large number of visionary leaders in this world who use the same three pillars in a reverse order, with the sense pillar first and the knowing pillar last. Some examples of people who have capitalized by using their sense pillar to access inspiration, and then using the feel pillar to explore if the inspiration feels right, and finally using the knowing pillar to put a tangible plan in place are not only the typical visionary leaders we always hear about such as Elon Musk, Richard Branson, Bill Gates, Jeff Bezos, and Steve Jobs. There are some extremely powerful women who have also used this skillset. One incredible example is the once homeless and now billionaire Zhang Xin from China, who built a real estate empire from poverty, using her sense pillar. Liberia's Leymah Gbowee is a mom of four who, without any experience in politics, was instrumental in rebuilding Liberia using out of the box insights and intuitions that brought people together and inspired peace. Through that, she received the Nobel Peace Prize in 2011. Finally, former IBM CEO Ginny Rometti is another leader who during her tenure used her sense pillar to spearhead the transformation of IBM from a computer sales company to the cloud-computing powerhouse it is today.

The lesson we can take away from this is that when we think we know what we know, we are only accessing 30 per cent of our wisdom as leaders. What sets a great leader and boss apart from an average, or even horrible one, is that a great leader is not satisfied with just knowing, but instead accesses their feeling and sensing pillars to develop a deeper sense of what they are thinking, so that they cannot just take the right decision, but also the wise decision.

Chapter 5

Four Steps to Being a WISE Leader

As discussed in the previous chapter, knowing is simply not enough for a boss. We must also be able to rely on our capacity to feel and sense so that we can access a deeper level of wisdom in everything we do. You might find yourself asking, 'So how do I access my wisdom as a leader?' You might also be thinking, 'How can I teach this concept to the people I work with?' These are questions I often receive from the leaders that I work with. To help them harvest more wisdom, I created a model that I would like to share with you too.

The model is called W.I.S.E. and stands for: 1. What's my blind spot? 2. Invite curiosity, 3. Surrender to my most unlikely teachers, and 4. Embrace uncertainty with possibility.

1. What's my blind spot?
    One of my most favourite rock songs of all time is the song 'Rockin' in the Free World' by Neil Young. The opening verse of this song has a very insightful observation where he says, 'There's colours in the street. Red, White, and Blue. People shuffling' their feet. People sleepin' in their shoes.' How many people are there who wake up every single day, get dressed, have breakfast, go to work, come home, eat dinner, and spend the rest of the evening in front of a TV, and that's what life looks like for them?

    One could question, is this really the best that life has to offer? Yet, in all likelihood, if you ask them, you might find that they are quite content with living this way, or possibly have resigned to the fact that this is what life has to offer them. Either way, the life they are living, and also the life you are living, is one that you have likely been practicing for many years. And because you've been practicing your daily rituals consistently for the past how many years of your life, they have become automatic. They have become you.

One very common example of automatic behaviour is from driving a car. I'm sure you've also been in a situation where you were driving home from work, the same way as you have been doing for years, and all of a sudden became aware that your mind had wandered off for a good chunk of time. The reason for this is that once a behaviour, action, or skill has been learned so well that it does not require conscious control, your brain conserves energy by shifting the task to less conscious areas of the brain that are less energy demanding. Even right now, as you are reading this book, there are many processes, thoughts, and attitudes that are going on the subconscious part of your brain that you have skilfully mastered because you have been practicing them for many years. In fact, you have practiced being this version of you so often in your life that you have become really good at it. Unfortunately, this also holds true for unfavourable habits, thoughts, and attitudes that might not be serving you very well and might even be holding you back from achieving greater success in life and at work.

The first step in accessing greater wisdom is to wake up to any self-inhibiting habits, rituals, attitudes, or thoughts that you have perfected in your life. In his book, *Language and the Pursuit of Happiness*, author and coach Calmers Brothers speaks about creating 'breaks in transparency'. What this means is that you look outward into the world using a lens that you have constructed over the course of your life, much like a window in your house, or the windshield of your car. Think about it. Imagine driving in your car and looking at the traffic ahead of you. If I were to ask you what you see, would your first thought be a windshield, or would your first thought be of the cars, the roads, traffic lights, side-streets, and so on? Yet, the quality and cleanliness of the windshield through which you are seeing traffic is going to determine how much of the traffic you can observe.

Your personal lens, through which you are observing your world, allows you to see your world, but the quality of that lens is going to dictate how much of yourself and how much of the world you are truly able to observe. Being aware that what you see is at the mercy of the quality of the lens you are looking through is critical in leadership.

Sticking with the analogy of driving a car, note that while you are driving, you also have mirrors. These mirrors allow you to see around you and behind you. In fact, those mirrors give you perspective. This perspective helps you when you decide to change lanes or turn a corner. When driving a car, what's the first rule we learn when we are about to change lanes? 'Check your blind spots!'

So, how can you add visibility and perspective to your job and life? Just like in driving, make sure you have a clean windshield that allows you to see clearly. Turn your head, look around for your blind spots, and, use your mirrors.

Who in your job or life can help you make sure you have a clean windshield through which you can see clearly and serve as your blind spot mirrors? Once you know the answer to that, you are ready for the next step in your pursuit of being a wise leader.

2.   Invite curiosity.

Have you ever met the Dalai Lama? I haven't. I'd love to one day, though. And if I ever did get to meet him, I'd likely have a million questions that I'd want to ask him. For starters, what does he eat for breakfast? Is he a vegan? Who does his wardrobe? Does he shave his head himself or are there people that help him with that? And I could go on and on.

You might be asking yourself, why is Marcel asking such shallow questions to one of the wisest people on this planet when he could be asking about how to attain enlightenment or something like that? Well, if that's your question, then I have sparked your curiosity too.

Your question about my lack of depth might trigger thoughts like, 'These shallow questions won't get Marcel anywhere. That's such a waste of time and intelligence. I hope Marcel never meets the Dalai Lama because he would just be wasting the Dalai Lama's time. Doesn't Marcel know that the Dalai Lama is an extremely busy person?' And if these are the types of thoughts that entered your mind, then your curiosity has left you.

Psychologists and philosophers have been fascinated by the concept of curiosity since the beginning of modern civilization. Socrates has been quoted saying, 'Wisdom starts in wonder.' Confucius once said, 'A man who asks a question is a fool for a minute, a man who never asks a question is a fool for a lifetime.' Einstein once said, 'Any fool can know, the point is to understand.' What they are all alluding to is that to think we know is in itself foolish, but to live in wonder and in an insatiable pursuit of more information toward understanding is the gateway to greater wisdom. Research in psychology is also confirming this. In 1994, psychologist George Loewenstein proposed that curiosity is a perceived gap between what we know and what we understand, which is still widely accepted today.

For some of us, curiosity can be a bit of an elusive animal that lives in an expansive world of possibilities, but is restricted by our subjective threshold of satiation for new information. What I mean by this is that the moment I think I know what I need to know about something or someone, I stop being curious. The human limitation to unlimited curiosity is not set in stone, but rather it is determined by how hungry we are to continue to learn something new or different about something or someone that we think we already know.

Going back to my example of my imaginary conversation with the Dalai Lama, with all of his wisdom that he has accumulated over the span of his fruitful life, do you honestly think he will let me ask him questions about what he likes to have for breakfast or who does his wardrobe? Absolutely not! In all of his wisdom, he is likely going to be more curious about me and my life, to a level of depth that shakes me to my core, than I could ever be about him. What sets the Dalai Lama apart from most of us is not his incredible knowledge, but rather his unrelenting curiosity about everything and everyone.

I remember having the most fascinating conversation with a friend of my wife's a few years back who told me about her experience meeting the Dalai Lama. Margie works for Air Canada in Toronto at Pearson International Airport where one of her jobs is to escort celebrities secretly from the airplane through customs and luggage collection. She is a spunky lady who has this incredible ability to only see good in people and situations. Margie is an amazing storyteller, and listening to Margie tell stories about her adventures or misadventures in life are better than any comedy movie you can think of. When Margie tells a story, you will be exposed to accompanying sound effects and physical re-enactments, including accents and voice imitations. I remember sitting in her kitchen with my wife and daughter, while she was feeding us constantly with her positive energy and food, another incredible trait of Margie's. During our visit, Margie turned to me and said, 'Marcel, guess who I met at the airport the other day? The Dalai Lama!' I was like, 'Woah, no way!' And she was like, 'Okay, this is the best story I need to share with you.' Margie then went into full blown animation mode and told me about her experience having to pick up the Dalai Lama from the airplane and escort him through customs. Her adventure with the Dalai Lama started when she had to try to get him off the airplane. Apparently, he had struck a conversation with some of the passengers and the crew in first class, and it took Margie forty-five minutes just to get him off the plane. But interestingly, the conversation he had nothing to do with leadership, mindfulness, fulfilment, meaning of life, or anything like that. Instead, he was interested in knowing more about everyone he was flying with, he just couldn't stop asking questions about them, about their lives, what they do, where they live, and so on.

Margie went on to say that after literally dragging the Dalai Lama off the airplane, it took them a whopping two hours to follow a route that normally takes less than twenty minutes to complete, just to get him from the airplane to where the private car would pick him up outside the airport, because he would stop to talk to literally everybody. She went on to tell me how the Dalai Lama was like a child, so curious, and wanting to speak to everyone, no matter who it was.

To Margie, this incredible act of curiosity started off as a bit of an annoyance because her task was to get him to his car, but after a while, she became so inspired by his act of curiosity, she just let go of any thoughts, judgments, or worries about getting him out on time, and just went with it.

She went on to explain that the walk from the airplane to the car was one she had done thousands of times before in her career, but she came to realize that after walking that same route for thousands of times, there were things that she had never noticed before. There were nooks and corners she had never paid attention to. There were people who were working at certain stations and stores that Margie had never stopped to get to know, even though she had worked there for thirty years.

Margie came to realize that what she thought she knew about her work was enough to be able to do her job, but through the Dalai Lama's act of curiosity, she came to realize that knowing enough to get the job done doesn't mean it's enough to feel satisfaction, wonder, and joy in what she was doing in her job.

The Dalai Lama's act of insatiable curiosity that day was an unintentional gift to her that taught her that the seemingly unimportant and mundane things in her life can actually offer her a tremendous opportunity for happiness and fulfilment, so long as she's willing to be open to approach them every day with the same sense of wonder and curiosity.

This is an example of how curiosity can be a gateway to wisdom, permitting we are willing to be hungry enough for information far above and beyond what we think we need to function in life.

As a leader and boss, take some time to think about your depth of curiosity in everything you do and the people you work with. If you exist in a space where you think you know enough about what you do, the people you work with, and what they are doing, you are robbing yourself, and your people, of the opportunity to explore that world of possibility, and thus, learn deeper and meaningful things that can serve you, your people, and your organization in ways you haven't even begun to imagine.

3.   Surrender to my most unlikely teachers.

Recently, I was called to a manufacturing company to help support the Chief Legal Officer, who had recently been promoted into this senior global leadership role from a regional one. In her performance review, some of the feedback that she had received from her staff was that she was difficult to work with and was extremely stubborn. Feedback from her Chief Operating Officer was that he felt that she didn't listen to her people and that she tended to be too forceful in her opinions. On top of that, the department's performance had seen a decline since my new client had taken office about one year earlier. The company wanted me to work with her to see if the coaching would help her develop a different mode of operating with her people.

In my first meeting with her, we met at her office to discuss her coaching that was being sponsored by the company. Arriving at the office fifteen minutes early, I took some time to sit in the lobby and take in the atmosphere to get a feel of the type of weather the office was experiencing. Sitting in the lobby, I noticed that the two receptionists were very busy working on processing incoming calls, and speaking very hastily to each other. As the employees of the company walked by, everyone walked like they were in a tremendous hurry. For the entire fifteen minutes, I saw many busy people scurrying around, but I did not see one smile. No laughter, no fun whatsoever. This place was all business. The feeling that I got was that this office had not seen sunshine in quite a while.

After waiting for a while, my client's personal assistant hurriedly came to get me at the lobby. She greeted me with a standard handshake and business smile, welcoming me to the office and ushered me to my client's office. She walked so fast, I actually had difficulty keeping up. As she quickly walked in front of me, passing through the different departments, I could observe the square cubicles where people were working, and everyone seemed to be severely busy. Again, there was no laughter or the appearance of anyone having fun. It was all business from where I was. When we got to my client's corner office, my client stood up and gave me a firm handshake and invited me to take a seat. After offering me coffee, she called her assistant and asked, 'Joanne, can we get two coffees in here?' Shortly after, Joanne came running in with two cups of coffee and silently put the cups of coffee in front of us. In none of those exchanges did I hear the words 'Please' or 'Thank you'. While taking the first sips of my coffee, I looked out of the window of this corner office and couldn't help but notice the incredible view of the city. I made a comment to her about the incredible view and her response was simply, 'Incredible view, but I'm usually too busy to notice.'

I turned my attention back to her and after a bit of small talk, I asked her about how she felt that I had been brought in as her coach. She told me that she was OK with having a coach and felt that she had always considered herself as being very coachable. I then asked her how she felt about her performance review. She told me that this was her first performance review as a Chief Legal Officer and that many of her staff members were very junior who did not yet understand how things worked in this company. She went on to explain that she had been with the company for almost twenty years and had learned that there was a certain way that things got done. With her staff being so young, they needed time to learn the ways of the organization. She was confident that next year's review would be very different, once her young staff members fell in line.

While she was explaining to me the 'ways of the company', I couldn't help but think about the strange, gloomy, depressed feeling I got sitting in the lobby. After she was done explaining the ways of the company to me, I leaned in for a moment and asked, 'On a scale of one to ten, how much do you enjoy being here?' She sat back for a moment and said, 'That's a strange question. Work doesn't need to be enjoyable; it just needs to get done.' I remained quiet and just kept leaning in and looking her in the eyes. 'Don't you think so?' she added. I let silence fill the room for a moment and then asked, 'Given the choice, would you prefer to work at a place where you had fun and felt great or where you felt indifferent?' 'Well, given the choice, I would prefer to work at a place where I enjoyed myself,' she said. I then asked, 'Who in this company will need to make that choice for you?' She sat with that for a moment and said, 'Well, that would be me, I guess.' After sitting with that for a little while, she looked at me and said, 'So, what you're saying is that I can either choose to keep things the way they are and have unhappy staff, or I could change things up and have happier staff working here.' I then asked, 'Which of these two options speaks to you the most?' 'Well, I do like the idea of having more fun and having an office that's more relaxed about things.' I then asked, 'Which of the two options would be most appreciated by your young staff members?' 'The fun option. But I've been working this way for so many years, I wouldn't know how to change,' she said. 'Who in this office, do you think, could teach you?' I then asked. She thought about that for a while and then asked, 'My staff, maybe?' 'How do you feel about that option?' I asked. 'Wow, that's tough. They are so young and have hardly any experience working here yet,' she answered. I let her sit with that comment for a moment, while she mulled over it in her mind. 'Maybe that's a good thing,' she said. 'What would they need from you, as their boss, to be able to teach you?' I asked. She sighed and said, 'I guess they would need my permission.' 'What would you need from yourself to give them that permission?' I asked. 'I guess, I'll need to give myself permission to be taught by people much junior than me.' She then sat back and smiled.

What my client realized through this interaction was that she was surrounded by teachers who all cared about how her department and the company were doing. Even by giving constructive feedback and sharing their grievances, these staff members are possible teachers, permitting the boss is ready to give them permission to teach her. Her ability to give that type of permission would mean that she would have to put aside her idea of how business gets done, put aside her twenty years of work experience, and instead have the courage to surrender to the teachings of people who are twenty years her junior.

In his book, *Mastery*, George Leonard explains that surrendering fully to the teachings of our teachers requires the complete removal of ego and letting go of what we believe we know.

In my client's case, her success as a boss would depend on her ability to let go of what she thought she knew about running her department and instead seek guidance from her staff members, no matter how junior they might be or how different their thoughts are from my client's.

With that newfound awareness, my client did prove to be extremely coachable and put her ego aside to start creating a more positive culture in the company. Six months later, I remember walking into a completely different office. Immediately upon entering the reception area, it seemed like the weather had changed to being so much sunnier inside. The reception team was smiling and was much more engaging with their visitors. Staff members inside the cubicle areas were laughing, and relaxing, and were notably having much more fun at work. Feedback from my client's COO was extremely positive and the performance of the team was climbing again.

What we can learn from this experience is that getting stuck with what we think we know and not giving others permission to teach us, even our most unlikely teachers, limits our capacity as bosses and leaders. So, as a boss, look around you and see if there are any unlikely teachers in your office. It could be the janitor, the receptionist, or it could be a co-worker or a manager whom you do not respect. Whoever it is, there will be potential teachers in your life whom you haven't given permission to teach you. What possibilities are you potentially missing out on by not giving them permission to teach you?

4.   Embrace uncertainty with enthusiasm.

A popular paraphrase that was inspired from Charles Darwin's book *The Origin of Species* is, 'It's not the strongest of the species that survives, nor the most intelligent. It's the one most adaptable to change.' Personally, I think this phrase became extremely relevant during the COVID pandemic. I know it did for me and for my business.

As I said in the introduction of this book, I really enjoyed my career where I got to travel to beautiful locations around the world, meeting extremely interesting leaders and their respective teams, before the pandemic hit in 2020, and like pretty much everybody else on this planet, I needed to make some serious adjustments.

Of course, my story is not unique. In fact, many business executives that I spoke to during the pandemic shared that they experienced the same benefits as I did. Many industries also benefitted from the pandemic. Online shopping, food delivery services, financial institutions, credit card companies, technology companies, and online web conferencing companies all saw massive increase in revenue over the course of the pandemic. In fact, in many of the companies that I continued to work with, a conversation grew whether or not to completely rethink the office of the future, as companies also learned that physical workspaces were no longer a necessity in many cases.

What I'm getting to here is that in the face of uncertainty, we humans have the capacity for amazing adaptability. Yet, simply having the capacity to see possibility during times of uncertainty doesn't mean it automatically happens with everyone. Psychologists have long identified that our ability to see possibility in times of uncertainty is limited by our individual levels of intolerance to uncertainty, also referred to as IU.

In their 2004 book, *Generalized Anxiety Disorder: Advances In Research and Practice*, Doctors Richard Heimberg, Cynthia Turk, and Douglas Mennin defined IU as 'the tendency to react negatively on an emotional, cognitive, and behavioural level to uncertain situations and events.' What this means is that we all have different tolerance levels in the face of uncertainty. In some of us, that tolerance may be low, resulting in constant stress, worry and anxiety; whereas in others, the tolerance can be high, resulting in the ability to see possibility and opportunity where others might not. In my opinion, this is a key factor that sets a great leader apart from a not so great one.

So, if a high tolerance to uncertainty—that is being able to maintain a positive mindset, to keep an open mind, and to embrace the possibilities in the unknown—would be considered ideal in leadership, a good question to ask is, 'Is tolerance to uncertainty trainable?' The short answer to that is yes. Over the past ten to twenty years, scores of research in the field of neuroscience has shown that we do have the capacity to create new neuro-circuits to help us master new skills and we also have the capacity to disrupt existing ones. One of the greatest discussions of recent times is not so much whether we can retrain our brains, but how we can retrain our brains to be able to tolerate uncertainty and see possibility instead. The general consensus today is that retraining our brains to see possibility in times of uncertainty is somewhat of a two-step process. Step one would be to train our brains to become more mindful, so that we can reduce the anxiety and fear related to uncertainty, and then step two would be to flex the neural muscles of possibility through daily practice.

In a 2018 paper in the journal *Organization Dynamics,* Professors Elizabeth King and Richard Badham from Macquarie Graduate School of Management wrote a very interesting article called 'Leadership in Uncertainty: The Mindfulness Solution.' In their paper, they proposed that the practice of mindfulness is a highly effective leadership strategy in times of uncertainty.

However, more than mindfulness meditation, which is a form of mental exercise that can help us become more mindful, King and Badham defined mindfulness as 'a quality or state of mind that attends to experience, avoiding or overcoming mindlessness by giving full and proper attention to presence, context and purpose.' What they, and other mindfulness experts, proposed was that mindfulness is a way of being that promotes awareness, attention, and acceptance, that in turn improves tolerance to uncertainty.

In the same paper, King and Badham proposed that mindfulness in the workplace works like a wheel starting with mindfulness of the individual which, with practice, becomes individual wisdom. Individual wisdom promotes mindfulness in others, creating collective mindfulness, which over time, translates into collective wisdom within the entire organization. In other words, wisdom is contagious.

By being more mindful of our experiences and ensuring that we can be fully present during times of challenge, we create an opportunity to maximize our tolerance to uncertainty by embracing our challenges in a mood of possibility and wonder.

What we can learn from this is that wisdom is an extremely powerful leadership skill that is certainly trainable. By using the W.I.S.E model, checking your blind spots, inviting curiosity, surrendering to your most unlikely teachers, and embracing uncertainty with enthusiasm, you will be able to reduce the dominance of your 'knowing pillar' and invite more 'feeling' and 'super-sensing' into how you lead and operate in life.

In the next chapter, we are going to explore how being a wise leader translates into Energy projection and Energy transfer, which will set the foundation of the Five Energies Framework.

Chapter 6

Energy Matters

In the introductory part of this book, I shared the story of my first experience of opening my own Energy pathways during one of my many memorable training sessions with the late Master Gobin while I was recovering from alcoholism in the military. In the first chapter, I then talked about my own experience of being a horrible leader and boss and how I had numerous experiences in my career where I was completely disconnected from my energy and myself. If you concluded from this that my relationship with Energy has not been a constant one, you would be correct. As I reflect back on my life, my relationship with Energy and Energy practice was nothing like Master Gobin, my karate teacher in Curacao, who was a dedicated Energy healer and who spent every day of his life perfecting the art of harnessing energy for greater performance and healing. For Master Gobin, his path was crystal clear to him, and he practiced his skills with purpose every day. I really admired that in him. His dedicated practice with energy spilled over into every aspect of his life and through that, he was more balanced, had incredible vitality, and was deeply connected to himself, his environment, and the people in his community. Just being in his presence would create an immense sense of calm and balance inside me, which was a polar opposite of how I would normally feel. And that connectedness I felt around him was something I wanted to feel all the time.

For me, however, the path towards connecting with my own energy was very different than Master Gobin. In the early half of my adult life, every positive experience I had of connecting with my Energy was more of an accident than it was a deliberate act. Despite the fact that I practiced martial arts for most of my life, practicing martial arts didn't naturally translate into greater energy in daily life. I also experienced the same with meditation. Even though I practiced meditation for most of my life, it never naturally translated over to greater mindfulness for me. I would feel great during the practice of either martial arts or meditation, but within a few hours, the effects of the exercise would wear off and I'd go back to being my regular, disconnected self.

Reflecting on this, I believe the reason why I had such a sporadic relationship with my own Energy was because I never fully trusted myself or trusted my Energy. Looking back at my own life's journey with Energy, I became most disconnected from myself and my energy when I got stuck in my head. For example, my many bouts with depression, my alcoholism, my ego while functioning as a 'fitness expert,' and moments of great stress were all times where I became completely dislodged from myself, my vitality, my intuition, my connectedness with myself and the world, and also my life's purpose.

On the other hand, those few times in my early adult life when I was able to fully connect with my energy and with myself were when I felt one with my energy and where I was in a state of flow. Those were the times when I would be practicing martial arts vigorously.

What I eventually learned from this is that in my case, Energy seems to be directly connected to my body that requires regular movement or exercise to flow freely. In times when I stop moving regularly, it feels like my body's Energy pathways gradually close. The more blocked my Energy pathways become, the more disconnected I begin to feel, which leads to feelings of being overwhelmed, anxiety, stress, and depression.

So, at this point, if you are asking yourself, 'What is this whole Energy thing and why don't I feel it?', you're not alone. Not feeling connected to your Energy is normal in most of us, at times. The beauty is that energy is there for you to tap into whenever you are ready. All it takes is a little trust and a little work on your body.

In my coaching work with professionals and leaders, I see in them a constant challenge to trust their Energy and intuition. Most of my clients start their journey struggling to trust something they cannot see or quantify. Of course, that's not surprising really. Let's face it, Energy seems to be one of those mysterious things that most of us can't define, but pretty much everyone can relate to.

For example, we know when it isn't present in us, when we feel low on energy, and we also know when it is available to us, when we feel we have a lot of energy. You may also have experienced someone at work who brought great energy to the team. Conversely, I'm also sure that you've experienced a few times at work where someone walked into the office and the energy in the room just seemed to disappear, leaving everyone in the room feeling like their life force had been sucked right out of them by some Energy vampire.

The truth of the matter is that energy is all around us and it is within us. Energy is everywhere. It is within all living beings and all non-living matter. It is present both in a physical sense as well as a non-physical sense. Even though this may be the case, our understanding of Energy and our relationship with it differs from culture to culture. To help you develop a greater appreciation of your energy and how to access it for yourself, let's explore the concept of energy from a scientific, as well as a philosophical, perspective.

Energy in the Western Science

In the Western science, energy is defined as 'the ability or capacity to do work,' a definition that stems from the age of Aristotle more than 2,000 years ago. Since the 17th century, Western scientists, in particular physicists, have been developing technologies and methodologies to gain a better understanding of physical energy. Over the past few hundred years, a general consensus between scientists has been that energy can't be created or destroyed but can only be transferred from one form to another. A simple example of transferring energy could be electromagnetic radiation from the sun that is converted into chemical energy through photosynthesis in plants. When we eat a salad, for example, that chemical energy stored in the salad is converted into other forms of energy in our bodies, such as potential energy in our muscles and chemical energy in our fat stores. Our daily functioning requires us to utilize the available energy which is within our bodies. It is then released back into the atmosphere through respiration and as heat energy.

An important note to make here is that the organ in the body that utilizes the most energy is the brain. As I mentioned in my previous book, *Headstrong Performance: Improve Your Mental Performance with Nutrition, Exercise, and Neuroscience*, even though the human brain only takes up 2 per cent of a person's bodyweight, it uses a whopping 20 per cent of the body's available energy. It has long been established that neurons in the brain communicate with one another through electrical impulses. These impulses produce so much electrical energy that if your brain had the right plug, you could charge your mobile phone with it.

Interestingly, the energy source for the brain is glucose and recent research has confirmed that the brain's glucose stores are not infinite. As glucose levels in the brain drop, so too does the brain's capacity to think and focus clearly, be empathetic toward others, apply self-awareness, and think strategically. What we can take away from this is that any leader or boss who aspires to lead with these qualities would need to ensure that sufficient energy is available in their brains.

Of significance here is that the regions of the brain most sensitive to energy availability are the structures responsible for inhibiting emotional and primal behaviours, areas that are involved in self-protection and survival. As availability of energy drops in the critical brain regions responsible for performing highly complex leadership tasks, energy stores in the more primal areas of the brain remain optimal, which opens the door for a loss of self-control and self-awareness, while also opening the door to possible emotional outbursts, distrust, and impulsivity.

Imagine what consequences this can have in work environments where the atmosphere is chronically gloomy or worse. In fact, research has shown that prolonged exposure to such work environments not only changes the brain's capacity to provide sufficient glucose to the self-regulatory centres in the brain, but those structures actually become thinner, thus losing their capacity for trust, empathy, and self-awareness altogether. In other words, making sure your brain has sufficient energy available is a critical leadership skill that should not be underestimated. So, what can you do to maximize energy in your brain? In my book *Headstrong Performance: Improve Your Mental Performance with Nutrition, Exercise, and Neuroscience*, I delve deeper into how you can optimize energy in your brain. In short, Energy can be maximized in the brain using two strategies. The first strategy is to engage in activities that increase Energy in the brain, such as exercise, a balanced diet, a sound sleep regimen, going out in nature, and regular mindfulness practice. The second strategy is to reduce the number of unnecessary activities that cost Energy, such as mindlessness, stress, multitasking, poor time management, and excessive screen time. Applying these two strategies simultaneously will greatly improve a positive energy balance in the brain and will help protect your brain, no matter how challenging life gets.

As you can see, Energy management from a Western science perspective is critically important, but in this case, the concept of Energy is limited to the physical world, where Energy is tangible and measurable. However, outside the Western science realm, many civilizations have a very different relationship with Energy, in particular the energy that is present in the non-physical world. Because this relationship with Energy is much older and holistic than in Western science, I prefer to refer to this as Holistic Energy Practices.

Energy in Holistic Practices

Early in my career in the fitness industry, in my pursuit to gain critical knowledge in my field, I enrolled into a university where I pursued a degree in Health Sciences, majoring in Complementary Medicine. In this program, my primary focus was the healing benefits of physical exercise. What I loved about this program was that it had a perfect blend of core courses in the Western sciences like pharmacology, pathophysiology, chemistry, and anatomy; but there were also courses that introduced me to other healing practices such as ayurvedic medicine that includes yoga from India, traditional Chinese medicine that includes qigong and tai chi, meditation, manual healing therapies, and other indigenous healing practices from around the world. This blend of Western and Holistic Healing classes really helped me develop an appreciation for the evolution of medical practice, both in the Western society and in the non-Western. However, with my focus being primarily on the healing power of exercise, I didn't pursue any of the healing arts until after I made my departure from the fitness industry as a fitness professional.

Not long after my departure from the fitness industry, I had a conversation with a friend about wanting to start studying martial arts again. She told me that there was someone that she felt I should meet, and she introduced me to a tai chi master named Master Zheng.

I met with Master Zheng at his home on the East Coast of Singapore. On a hot and humid Tuesday evening, which is typical in Singapore, Master Zheng was teaching tai chi to a handful of his students and he invited me to join to do a trial session. I naively accepted his invitation. In my arrogance, I believed that my many years of studying martial arts would be an advantage and I would at least not look like a total idiot while trying to learn yet another martial art. Well, my years of experience didn't help. My years of studying the hard arts of martial arts had engrained a habit of tension in my body that rendered me completely useless in tai chi.

Tai chi as a form of martial arts is practiced while being completely relaxed in a way that promotes the flow of Qi, or life energy through the body that is believed to have unprecedented power. It can be used as a healing power, but also as a destructive power to overcome an attack from another person.

During my session, I felt myself becoming increasingly frustrated with myself as my body was just not allowing me to relax into the exercises. After the session, Master Zheng came up to me and asked me about my experience. I mentioned to him that I didn't think tai chi was for my body. He looked at me deeply and said, 'What did you expect?' I told him that with my martial arts experience, I should have been able to do better. His answer was simple, but profound. He said, 'Qi can only flow if you are prepared to let go.' I thought about that for a moment and came to the conclusion that in my tai chi lesson, I was being resistant to learning something different. Instead, I was telling myself that I wanted to learn something new, while at the same time, I was not giving myself permission to only be a student. I was trying to hold on to my expert's ego while attempting to learn something new and that did not work. If I wanted to study tai chi, I had to be prepared to surrender to the teachings of Master Zheng and let go of everything I thought I knew about martial arts.

Opening myself up to learning the soft art of tai chi did not come easy. Learning to relax while practicing a defensive move did not come easy. Learning to relax while being powerful seemed counterintuitive and was against everything that I thought I knew about martial arts. I quickly realized that if I wanted to explore a completely different way of being a martial artist, I had to give myself permission to be vulnerable. Yet, old habits of my old warrior mindset resisted this new way of being immensely. Over time, with much patience and humility, I slowly learned to let go of my inner tension and learned to surrender to the teachings of Master Zheng. And it was during one of our lessons that he introduced me to the power of Qi, or life force.

In this session, I was practicing a sparring exercise with Master Zheng called Push Hands. In this exercise, two tai chi practitioners stand opposite each other where their hands or arms are in constant contact with the hands or arms of the training partner. The idea of the exercise is that both practitioners move their bodies and arms in a way so as to disbalance the opponent without striking them and while remaining completely relaxed. In my push hands exercise with Master Zheng, he masterfully toyed with every single advance I would make to disbalance him.

No matter whether I rotated, pushed with my left or with my right arm, his body and arms flowed like water around my advances. With every failed advance, I felt myself becoming more frustrated and with my frustration came tension. Eventually, I became so tense, Master Zheng would just rotate his body and I would find myself falling forward.

Sensing my frustration, he stopped the exercise and told me how he could sense the tension building up, and just waited for me to push myself over. I asked him, 'How can I push someone over while being completely relaxed? We need force to push someone over.' He smiled and said, 'Let's do it again.' I tried to pull myself together and, going into the exercise, tried to relax as much as possible.

It didn't take long before I started feeling the tension build up in my body again, but this time, Master Zheng didn't push me out of balance, he did something remarkable. At one point, I thought I had an opening and reached for his left upper arm with my right hand to push him over. Instead of deflecting, this time Master Zheng allowed me to make contact, but as I did, it was like pushing against a brick wall. His stance was firm and so deeply grounded that his body did not move, no matter how hard I tried to push.

Looking in his eyes, I could see he was completely relaxed, yet his body was incredibly heavy. And then, in an instance, he rotated his hip and released an audible grunt that came from so deep down in his bowels, it was like nothing I had heard before. With this one twist and grunt, I felt a wave of energy hit me right in the chest, which threw me six feet back and knocked me off my feet. Sitting on my ass, completely stunned, I had just been schooled in the power of Qi, that can only be harnessed when we are relaxed.

I learned that night from Master Zheng that there is a universe of knowledge and wisdom out there that I hadn't even begun to explore, let alone understand. And if I wanted to learn more about this incredible energy, I would need to give myself permission to stop relying strictly on the pillar of knowing, but to also explore the pillars of feeling and sensing, which is where Qi can be harnessed.

Unlike the Western sciences, where the distinction of Energy is generally restricted to the physical sciences, other cultures have a much longer and more holistic, and often a spiritual relationship with Energy that goes back ages before any awareness of Energy in the Western cultures. Ancient cultures across most of the continents, such as the Egyptians in ancient Egypt with the worship of the sun, Indians in ancient India and their incredible Sanskrit texts, the Chinese, the Japanese, Native Americans, Australian aboriginals, and African tribes, all shared a common understanding that everything in this world and universe is connected through Energy. Despite the fact that all of these cultures were separated by time and geography, they all seem to have come to that same conclusion that Energy is the binding force that connects us all with each other and every single thing in the universe.

One of the most ancient written references to this common understanding of Energy goes as far back as almost 5,000 years ago in ancient Egypt, where it was believed that all people contained Ka, a life force or energy. Old Sanskrit texts from India from 4,000 years ago make reference to Prana, or life-force, that connects everything and everyone in the universe. Ayurvedic medicine, for example, is a natural form of healing that arose from the same Sanskrit texts thousands of years ago and is still practiced today. Ayurvedic medicine uses the understanding that we have a number of energy centres, or *chakras*, within us. Our chakras absorb the energy from the universe, while also projecting energy back into the universe in a constant cyclical process. Yoga, which originated in India at around the same time as ayurvedic medicine, was originally evolved as a way of being in body, mind, and spirit that harmonizes the yoga practitioner with the universe. That way of being included forms of physical exercise, meditation, and spiritual practices that evolved into the practice of yoga as we know it today. Of particular interest for this book is that maintaining a healthy flow of energy between our chakras is not only an important indication of health, it is also critical in managing the type of energy we project onto others and the universe. According to ayurvedic and yogic practices, our internal environment and the alignment of our chakras dictate the type of energy we project and the type of impact we have on our immediate environments. This Energy projection is known as an aura. Each type of aura is represented as a colour. Some colours are very open, empathetic, and wise, whereas other colours represent a lighter and more fun loving energy. In contrast to this, there are auras that are very strong willed, forceful, and authoritative in nature. There are also auras that are extremely grounded and detail orientated.

A similar concept to Prana evolved in China approximately around the same time, 4,000 years ago. In China, this life force was named Qi and became the foundation for what we know today as traditional Chinese medicine, or TCM. Similar to ayurvedic medicine, TCM operates on the understanding that the flow of Qi is balanced through the body. An interesting evolution in the history of the application of Qi is the understanding that Qi arises from the interplay between yin and yang. Much like the two opposite sides of a coin, the positive and the negative charge in a battery, or the difference between night and day, the one cannot exist without the other creating a perfect flow of Energy through the interplay between both yin and yang. Much like the Indian concept of Prana, the flow of yin and yang is what connects everything in this universe together. Yin can be described as the receptive or inviting state, whereas yang is the active or determined state.

Much like in India, where practitioners developed yoga to maximize their energy, in China, practitioners developed qigong, which consists of a series of breathing, meditative, and physical exercises that maximize the flow of Qi in the body. From this practice, the martial arts kung fu and tai chi chuan evolved, with kung fu being the hard style for physical fitness and combat purposes, and tai chi chuan as the soft style for inner balance, health, and longevity.

Many practitioners of tai chi chuan also practice the qigong exercises and vice versa; also many practitioners practice all three for overall vitality. In my own practice of tai chi chuan, I also incorporate qigong exercises.

Interestingly, it was during my practice of tai chi chuan that I began to see similarities in human behaviour in the workplace represented in yin and yang. To exert influence over their people, some leaders would by default adopt a yang stance, or apply yang energy, that was forceful, authoritative, and determined, while I would see other leaders apply more of a yin energy to be more passive and receptive to ideas and perspectives from others.

Neither one of those Energy choices proves to be the ideal energy in every situation, of course. Different situations require different energies. Every once in a while, ever so rare, I would have the privilege of witnessing poetry in motion when I get to see a leader naturally adopt either the yin energy or the yang energy as per the situation. The end result was always extremely powerful. This is what inspired me to develop this understanding into a practical model for leaders to learn how to shift their energy, so that they can be more effective in collaboration, teamwork, delegation, and negotiation.

In the upcoming chapters, we will explore each of these energies in greater depth and you will have the opportunity to start practicing using the different energies in different situations.

Western science meets Asian philosophy

I started this chapter off with a bit of a dualistic approach, showing a contrast between how Western science approaches the concept of energy and pretty much every other culture out there in the world. For a large part, that separation was created in history due to Western science's inability to see and measure Energy in its non-physical form. However, over the past 100 years or so, with the advances in technology, Western scientists have been developing, and are still developing, new technologies that are slowly making visible that which, until recently, was invisible and thus measurable. Coming from a Western science educational background while also being heavily influenced by Asian philosophies, I find this particularly exciting. Slowly but surely, Western science is proving what many cultures have believed and known for thousands of years.

Since the late 19th century, Western science has used technology to measure electrical currents in the human body. A few popular technologies are the electrocardiogram to measure heart function, and the electroencephalogram to measure brain waves.

Since then, a number of scientists have taken a key interest in bioelectronics, measuring the electrical energy in the body, and bioelectromagnetic science that studies the interactions between magnetic fields within, but also between, organisms.

In a recent paper written by Doctor Christina L. Ross and published in the medical journal *Global Advances in Health and Medicine*, Dr Ross notes that in recent history Western or allopathic medicine traditionally used bioelectronics for diagnostic purposes and would then transition to biochemical medicine, such as drugs for treatments. However, we are now starting to see an emergence of Energy medicine, which has been defined as a branch of integrative medicine that studies the science of therapeutic applications of subtle energies to bring the body's collective systems, such as the cardiovascular, the endocrine, the muscular, the neurological, the skeletal systems, and so on back into balance.

In short, Energy medicine helps us understand how all of the systems of the body are connected, and are in constant communication through the subtle vibrations they make. Research is showing that when the systems are healthy and in harmony, the vibrations of all of our organs and systems create a symphony of energy that can be clearly recognized and recorded. This symphony of vibrations creates an energy field known as the Human Energy Field, or HEF in short.

In contrast, when certain systems in the body are not in harmony, for example, because of disease, poor health, lack of sleep, or stress, the symphony becomes deregulated, resulting in a dramatic change in the HEF. In other words, when we don't take care of ourselves, our bodies' symphonies begin to play a dramatically different tune. This vibrational tune can be recorded using technology that is available to us today. Measuring and recording HEF is a powerful alternative diagnostic tool for diagnosing the onset of disease.

What's even more fascinating is that recent research is also showing that upon subjecting a person or animal with a deregulated HEF to coherent energy patterns, such as polarity therapy, vibration therapy, acupuncture, healing touch therapies, and so on, the dysregulated HEF begins to turn back to normal, resulting in a boost in immune function, which then aids in the healing process against disease.

What this means is that when we humans are not OK, whether it's in body or mind, our bodies begin to transmit energy in a different way and this can be received and measured. At the same time, when we humans are exposed to balanced energy vibrations, these vibrations trigger within our own bodies and minds a shift back to a state of harmony and balance.

What is significant about HEF is that western science is catching up to help us better understand the human aura that is created by the chakras in ayurvedic medicine as well as our understanding of yin and yang, and Qi from traditional Chinese medicine.

Even more encouraging for these ancient healing arts is the fact that rapid developments in modern research is helping us identify where the chakras and Qi might be positioned in the body, moving them away from some mystical invisible theory into tangible structures within the body. For example, by measuring the energy fields produced by the endocrine system in our bodies, the system that modern medicine describes as responsible for all hormonal processes, new research is beginning to suggest that the endocrine system and the Chakras are actually one and the same, and that the endocrine system plays a much more complex role in the HEF than just producing hormones.

Similarly, recent advances in research are also helping researchers identify what Qi might be and where the Qi meridians, through which Qi flows, might be in the body. Even though not enough research has been conducted to fully prove or disprove the existence of Qi meridians and Qi flow, researchers in Korea have spent the past few decades attempting to identify and explain Qi in western terms. Their own research-backed theory, that has been evolving for the past fifty years, is that a previously unrecognized system called the primo vascular system, or PVS, exists in the body. What's interesting about this concept is that the proposed PVS is a connective system that integrates the cardiovascular, nervous, immune, and hormonal systems through the electromagnetic waves, originating from within the spiralling DNA of each cell, creating not only electromagnetic energy, but also a transport system for generational DNA knowledge and wisdom that connects all living organisms and the environment.

Energy projection in leadership

OK, so now that we have delved a little deeper into the science of Energy in both Eastern and Western cultures, let's take a closer look at how energy can play a part in leadership.

A famous western researcher who has spent the past fifty years expanding our understanding of Energy beyond the physical realm is Doctor Bruce Lipton, author of the bestselling book *The Biology of Belief: Unleashing the Power of Consciousness, Matter & Miracles*. As a cellular biologist at Stanford University's School of Medicine, Doctor

Lipton discovered that the outer membranes of all of our cells function like antennae that receive vibrations from the environment and then relay that information to the DNA of our cells in such a powerful way that the vibrations actually change the structure of our DNA. These structural changes can be so profound that they even carry over onto our offspring, so our future generations are more prepared to be able to survive in the environment they are born into.

Remember that I mentioned earlier how through the vibrations from our HEF, we each play a different tune and that when we are not well, for example, the vibrations change to create an alternate tune? Well, what we can learn from Doctor Lipton's research is that as a leader, the type of tune your vibrations play has a direct impact on the people in your environment.

The vibration receptors in every cell of their bodies and minds will respond to the tune you are playing, and that tune, whether it's positive or negative, will have a direct impact on how they feel and operate.

As a leader and boss, your Energy projection, has a dramatic impact on the DNA, the cells, the bodies, and the minds of your people. And all of that happens without you even needing to say a word. How powerful is that?

Well, let's take that a step further. Your presence and the vibration tune you are playing not only change the DNA of your people, but even the DNA of their children. The impact of how you show up every single day can leave a genetic legacy that is felt for generations.

So, in closing, we started this chapter looking at energy in the physical world through the eyes of traditional Western science. We then explored the Eastern philosophies and their understanding of energy as it relates to the chakras, Qi, and yin and yang. We then finished with some blending of Western science with Eastern philosophy to help solidify the understanding that we are all connected by energy and that as a leader, how you show up and the energy you are projecting has a profound impact on the people in your work and life, and even their future offspring.

So, right now, you might be asking yourself, 'So, what can I do to make sure I am projecting energy in a way that has a positive effect on my people and their kids?' To help you answer that question, I'm going to share with you a framework to help you do just that. In this framework, I will share with you the five energies and the accompanying postures in the next chapter.

These five energies were inspired in me through my introductions with ayurvedic medicine and the chakras while studying Complementary Medicine, my practice as a martial artist, in particular tai chi and qigong, and also my training in executive coaching. There are two coaching modalities that have helped me solidify and validate this framework for myself that I would like to highlight. The ground-breaking work done by my friends at the Newfield Network and also the pioneering work done by the Strozzi Institute in the United States.

Both of these organizations have done tremendous work spanning decades in the fields of leadership and coaching to help give coaches and clients clearer distinctions around the intricate synergies of body, emotion, and language. Thanks to their collective influence and guidance during my own training, I was able to build a user-friendly framework for incorporating energy work into my practice as a coach that I still use today.

Chapter 7

Introducing the Five Energies

As I mentioned in the previous chapter, my first introduction to the Chinese use of the five energies as a framework was when I started practicing tai chi and qigong. In class, under Master Zheng's guidance, we would practice a series of movements that consisted of perfectly synchronized stances, breathing patterns and arm movement patterns to improve physical and mental health. These qigong movements are often referred to as wuxing qigong.

Wuxing can be loosely translated as the 'Five Phases.' They found their origin thousands of years ago in Taoist philosophy and traditional Chinese medicine.

The Five Phases philosophy focuses on the five elements of nature viz. metal, water, earth, wood, and air and their connectedness through energy. Not to be confused with the four elements of matter in Western science—earth, fire, water, and air—the Five Phases don't actually consist of their named matter, but rather, each name represents an Energy or a concept.

Historically, wuxing have been used to describe the relationships between pretty much everything, from the cosmos, the planets, and the earth, to the relationships between our organs to promote health, as used in traditional Chinese medicine, to the seasons of the year, to the directions, and even the relationships between people.

In tai chi and qigong, the wuxing are used to not only promote health, but also to describe strategic steps in the art of negotiation, collaboration, influence, and combat and conflict resolution. It would not come as a surprise that, arguably the most quoted Asian military strategist, Sun Tzu, relied on his understanding of wuxing to develop some of his most famous military strategies that focused on winning wars through relationships rather than the use of force.

In my years studying martial arts, I was always fascinated by Sun Tzu's incredible wisdom and how he used his knowledge of human nature and Taoist philosophy to become one of the most powerful military leaders of all time. But it wasn't until I was introduced to tai chi and qigong that I really began to develop a deep appreciation for wuxing, how this understanding can help us know ourselves, the people we work with, and help us develop nonviolent modes of communication that allow us to be a positive influence in other people's lives.

In her book, *The Five Archetypes: Discover Your True Nature and Transform Your Life and Relationships*, ayurvedic nutritionist and reiki master, Carey Davidson, explains that each element of the wuxing can also represent a certain personality or archetype who exhibits specific behavioural tendencies. For example, a person with predominantly a 'Wood' personality will likely be confident, driven, and courageous. A person with predominantly a 'Fire' personality will likely be enthusiastic and a great communicator. An 'Earth' personality will likely be more balanced, nurturing, and stable, a 'Metal' personality will be more stoic, detail-oriented, and patient, whereas a 'Water' personality might be more cautious and conservative.

An interesting differentiator from popular personality tests that are used in organizations to help professionals better understand how their personalities are driving their behaviours, the wuxing five elements are strongly linked with traditional Chinese medicine or TCM. From this perspective, the five elements archetypes are not seen as personalities that drive certain behaviours, but rather that the personalities are driven by the energy balance in the body and the mind.

What I love about this philosophy is that our personalities are not fixed, which many people might think, but rather that our personalities are fluid, depending on our health, well-being, and our energy balance. This makes total sense when you think about it. Imagine having a bad headache and having to attend a meeting. How much effort would it take you to be enthusiastic and upbeat during that meeting? Which archetype would show up for you while you are having that intense headache? In all likelihood that archetype would be different from your usual archetype.

From a leadership perspective, this means that we are not victims of the personality types that we were born with. Instead, based on this perspective, if we can master our Energy, we have the power to shift our personalities, so that we can be more effective in how we lead and function while working with others.

This is where the Energy work in tai chi is so extremely powerful. By mastering how we harness, utilize, and project energy, we can learn to master how we can shift from one of the five archetypical elements to the next, so that we can become more effective and more adaptable in how we lead and how we perform.

Inspired by the wuxing, yin-yang, and the Indian chakras, I have created a functional model that helps us understand ourselves and our people in a more digestible way. Rather than using the wuxing elements

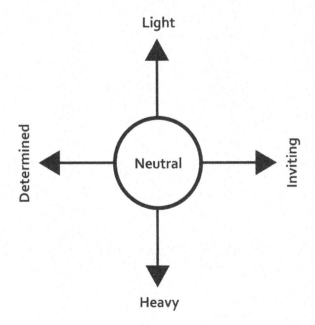

archetypes or the chakras to describe the energies and related postures, I use a more descriptive terminology to help speed up the understanding of the energies. These five energies are: Determined Energy, Inviting Energy, Light Energy, Heavy Energy, and finally, Neutral Energy.

To help you visualize how these Energies work in relationship to each other, I want you to imagine a four-point compass with arrows pointing towards east and west on the horizontal axis and arrows pointing towards north and south on the vertical axis. The west-pointing arrow is the forward or outward moving energy that is pushed into the environment. Think of pushing against a heavy object, like shifting a filing cabinet, or pushing a person in a certain direction. There is a determined effort required when pushing something or someone in a direction that you want them to go. If the west-pointing arrow is yang, then the east-pointing arrow will be yin, the opposite. So, rather than pushing energy out, which the west-pointing arrow does, the east-pointing arrow draws energy in. It is inviting in nature. In this situation, rather than pushing an idea, perspective, or vision into the world, the east-pointing arrow will invite ideas, perspectives, or vision from others.

The north and south-pointing arrows function similar to the yin and yang way. The arrow pointing north points towards the sky. It is connected to the cosmic energy of the universe and that energy is light in nature, much like a helium balloon. Imagine the balloon being tied to the crown of your head, or your crown chakra. As the balloon inflates with cosmic energy, it will rise up into the air and gently lift you off the ground. Being in a state of Light Energy, life feels less serious. It's a state where joyfulness, creativity, spontaneity, and playfulness live. On the opposite end of Light Energy is the south-pointing arrow that points toward the ground. The opposite of light, of course, is Heavy. Heavy Energy connects to the earth energy and is extremely grounded. Like the roots of a tree, it provides us with stability, certainty, safety, and sensibility.

One energy we have not discussed yet is Neutral Energy. Neutral Energy sits right at the middle, where the other four energies intersect. Neutral Energy is neither forward moving nor inviting, nor is it light or heavy. It is Neutral.

So, let's take a closer look at each of the energies as they apply to you and leadership. Before we do so, remember that we project all five of the energies throughout our day, in different situations and scenarios. What's critical here is to begin to develop an understanding of how these energies show up for you in those situations. Once you are more aware of how these energies show up for you, you will also start becoming aware of how you might be projecting these energies toward other people and situations. With this awareness, you can start learning how to master the energy you project, so that you can start using this awareness as a tool to serve you better in how you get things done and in how you lead.

So, how might these energies show up for you? Well, over the past ten years working with hundreds of professionals, I can say that we all tend to have our own unique experiences with our energies. So, identifying how these energies show up for you will likely be unique to you and it will become evident over time and with more practice. Rather than focusing on how they might show up right now, before you have even begun experimenting with them, let's focus on where they might show up for you.

In your body

In his bestselling—and for me, life-changing—book *The Power of Now: A Guide to Spiritual Enlightenment*, Eckhart Tolle says that consciousness does not live in the mind, but rather, it lives deep within the body. He explains that when your mind takes up all of your attention, you are no longer in your body, and thus further removed from consciousness and your being. Therefore, to become conscious of how you are showing up in different situations, you must be able to redirect your attention away from what's going on in your mind and shift it back into your body.

I mentioned earlier that when I redirect my attention away from my body and live too much in my own head, I relapse into my depression, but when I can keep my attention in my body, like when I'm exercising or practicing martial arts, I can keep my depression at bay. Of course, this doesn't mean that when you want to bring your attention into your body, you need to start doing push-ups. However, if you struggle to bring your attention into your body, like what happened with me and my depression, then exercising could be a great way to practice bringing your awareness into your body.

So, what does awareness into the body actually look like? Well, that really depends on the type of observer you are. We all have our own unique relationships with our bodies. Some of us are extremely in tune with how our bodies feel and move at any giving moment. Others, on the other hand, may struggle with feeling how our bodies are feeling in any given situation. Either way, it is possible to bring your attention into your body. Here's a tip! The moment you find yourself asking the question, 'What am I feeling right now?' or 'Why can't I feel my body?', your attention is no longer in your body, but it has shifted into your mind. The trick is to observe with the intent to observe and not to diagnose, judge, understand or rationalize. Earlier, I jokingly mentioned doing push-ups to bring attention into the body. Push-ups as a thought scenario is very fitting in this case. Imagine yourself doing push-ups as an exercise. When you start your set of push-ups, you might feel the weight of your body shift onto your hands as you get into your push-up position. Imagine feeling that weight on your arms. Feel how your arm muscles tighten up to take the weight of your body. Feel how the palms of your hands are pressed into the ground. Imagine feeling the texture of the floor. Are you on a wooden floor, a carpet, a yoga mat, on the sand on a beach, or somewhere else? Feel that texture! As you commence your first push-up, you feel your arms bending at the elbow and you feel your body lower toward the ground. As your body gets closer to the ground, you can feel the muscles in your arms, chest, core, and legs contracting to keep your body nice and straight. While you are lowering your body, inhale and feel the air enter into your airways and into your lungs. Notice how your chest cavity expands while you inhale. From the bottom of your push-up, you forcefully push yourself back up into your starting position. Feel how your muscles contract forcefully and how your arms straighten. During the pushing up phase, exhale forcefully through your mouth, notice how your chest deflates, and how the warm air from your lungs passes through your throat and mouth into the air. This would be an example of doing a push-up with the attention on the body.

On the other hand, I might find my attention shifting away from my body while doing the push-ups, when I catch my inner voice saying things like, 'Oh, I feel heavy today. I shouldn't have eaten that second slice of cheesecake last night,' or, 'All right, I promised myself I would do twenty push-ups today. This was one, only nineteen more to go.' Both of these stories from my inner voice are examples of me shifting my attention away from my body. Of course, this is just an example, but training yourself to observe your body, just like in this push-up example, is a great way to practice shifting your attention into your body.

In a similar fashion as with the push-ups example, you can start practicing paying attention to certain processes that are happening in relation to the energy you are experiencing. Whether you are projecting Determined, Inviting, Light, Heavy, or Neutral Energy, or whether you find yourself responding to the energy of someone else, you can use your attention to these processes as a means to guide you to help you understand what energy you might be embodying. Here are a few observations that I like to focus on to help keep my attention into my body. I'm sure there are many more observations you can make. These tend to work very well for me:

1. Bodyweight: Does my body feel heavy, or light in this situation?
2. Muscles: Do my muscles feel tight and contracted, or relaxed and expanded?
3. Vision: Can I see what is in my peripheral field, or do I have laser point focus?
4. Shoulders: Are my shoulders pulled up to my ears, or sitting loosely on my body?
5. Chest cavity: Is my chest open and expanded, or caved in and contracted?
6. Heart: Is my heart rate rapid and loud, or is it slow and quiet?
7. Stomach: Do I feel a knot in my stomach, or is it relaxed?
8. Legs: Do my legs feel heavy, or do they feel limber?

9. Jaw: Does my jaw feel clenched and tight, or does it feel relaxed?
10. Face: Is my facial expression serious and tight, or open and joyful?

I invite you to practice bringing more awareness into your body in different situations throughout your day. You might find that your body responds very differently in all of the situations that you find yourself in during your day. For the sake of practice, take a few seconds in each situation of your day to observe your body. Below are some situations where you could practice observing your body:

1. When you wake up in the morning,
2. When you are getting ready for work,
3. While you are commuting to work,
4. When you first step into your workplace,
5. When you see and greet different colleagues,
6. When you see your boss,
7. At the beginning, middle, and end of each meeting or presentation,
8. At the end of a long day,
9. When you get home at night and see the people you love,
10. When you lay your head on your pillow after a long day.

Remember, that if you find your inner voice creating some form of dialogue about what you might be experiencing, such as, 'Oh my gosh, I'm so tired this morning,' or 'Today's going to be an awesome day and I can't wait to get to work', your attention has shifted away from your body. If you catch your attention shifting away from your body, that's totally fine. It's not a requirement to keep your attention on your body all day long. That would not be practical. However, when you do find your inner voice speaking to you, take advantage of that inner voice and explore how the language from your inner voice is affecting the state of your body.

In your mind

Even though Eckhart Tolle mentioned how true consciousness lives with our attention in the body, that doesn't take away from the fact that we do spend a lot of time in our own heads. In 2020, researchers at Queens University in Canada used functional MRI to observe the brains of people in thought. What they discovered was that the average adult has around 6,200 thoughts per day. That's a lot of thinking. The truth is, as humans, we spend a lot of time inside our own heads. On top of that, the human mind doesn't only consist of thoughts, it also consists of memories, feelings, emotions, moods, and perceptions. This soup of mental processes makes up the framework from which we view our experiences within our world. Through those experiences, each of us forms our own assessments about our experiences, which then becomes our beliefs, biases, opinions, passions, and mindsets.

An interesting interplay that really had an impact on my depression was the relationship between my emotions, moods, and my thoughts. Those times when I found myself stuck in my depression, my depressed mood would make it virtually impossible for me to think positive thoughts. Interestingly, those negative thoughts, fuelled by a depressed mood, would also limit my ability to notice anything positive happening in my environment or the world. No matter how hard I would try, seeing the upside in anything seemed impossible. In my depressed mood, I observed and experienced my world from a glass-half-empty perspective. What's scary is that the glass-half-empty perspective was real for me. There was no other option. There was no glass half empty because there was no glass half full. In my depressed state, what I experienced was my reality. It was in my mind, the way that it was. The certainty that my life was restricted to being nothing more than pain, suffering, and misfortune was so scary, it drove me even further into my depression, creating a perfect loop of self-imposed doom, that eventually led to thoughts of suicide a number of times in my young life.

Since then, I have learned that we all function with an operating system that gives us the capacity to either shape our lives into a life of positive experiences that is full of opportunities for growth, learning and abundance, or like how I experienced it, shape our lives in the opposite way.

Whether you like it or not, your mind's operating system is always working, even while you are reading this book. It doesn't only show up in your thoughts, but it also shows up in your body, as we mentioned earlier, and also shows up in the way you are projecting energy.

Much like how we practiced learning to observe your body, it's also a good practice to learn to observe your moods, emotions, beliefs, biases, opinions, and mindsets. Some questions you can ask yourself while you are observing your mind is:

1. What am I feeling right now? Am I feeling happy, sad, angry, frustrated, fearful, etc.?
2. What is my mood? Am I grateful, resentful, accepting, tired, energetic, enthusiastic, etc.?
3. Is what I am thinking simply my opinion or is it a fact?
4. Am I open to hearing other opinions and perspectives that I don't share?
5. What am I prepared to do to prove myself wrong?

While you are asking yourself these questions, remember that you are still inside your own mind. None of these questions have manifested themselves into the external world. The beauty of thought is that it is also a wonderful place to practice new ways of thinking, perceiving, believing, feeling, and so on. While you are doing this exercise, try to expand your observation into your body and see how your body responds to your own conversation in your own mind.

In your actions and inactions

Even though there must be as many definitions of leadership as there are leaders, my favourite leadership quote is from John Quincy Adams who said, 'if your actions inspire others to dream more, learn more, do more, and become more, you are a leader.' What I personally love about this quote is that it implies that a leader need not be someone who was hired into senior management position, but rather could be anyone within the organization who acts in a way that inspires people. As a leader, whether you are a leader of an organization, a team, or a parent, your actions and inactions matter to those who observe you, even when you think nobody is looking. Ultimately, how you act, or how you don't act, will be observed by others who will either be inspired by you, or demotivated by you.

In my coaching with leaders, I have learned that when it comes down to actions, there are three primary categories: big actions, small actions, and inactions. Big actions are those decisions, actions, and conversations that are of great significance to you as a leader and that may have a major impact on you, your people, and your organization. These big actions happen every day and within the scope of those actions, you are most likely very present and probably exemplary. In most conversations I have with my senior leaders, if I were to ask them to give me examples of moments when they displayed actions of great leadership, they generally mention examples that can be classified as big actions.

The second category includes the small actions. These are the daily habits and rituals that you are not consciously aware of. Some examples can be whether or not you habitually use the words 'please' and 'thank you' when speaking to anyone within your organization, whether you glance at your phone while someone is speaking to you, whether you stand still and look someone straight in the eye when they try to speak to you, whether you thank people for sharing their ideas and perspectives even if you disagree with them, and so on. Many of these habits and rituals are so deeply ingrained in our subconsciousness that we are mostly not aware of how we are present in those situations. Interestingly, you will have many more small actions in a day than you will have big ones, and it's the small ones that will make or break a leader over time.

The final category is inaction. What I mean by inaction is either your conscious decisions to not act or your inaction due to a lack of consciousness or visibility. For example, a conscious decision to not act could be when you are asked to do something that is against your values and you refuse. Of course, someone could argue that a declaration to not act, making a conscious decision, or even a making a choice, in themselves are actions. I would not disagree with that at all. The distinction between whether a decision is an action or inaction is not really of relevance in the context of energy projection. What's more critical here is the understanding of how a conscious decision to not act can show up for you in your body, in your mind, and in the way you project your energy. For example, what is your inner voice telling you when you choose to make such a decision to not act? How does the decision to not act show up for you in your body? And finally, what type of energy are you projecting as a result of the interplay between your mind and body in that situation?

More significantly than a conscious decision to not act are the many inactions in our day that are either due to a lack of visibility or a lack of consciousness. As a leader, having visibility is critical. However, you are only human, and humans are limited in their capacity to see what they do not pay attention to. That is not your fault; it's how your brain is designed. Our brains can only see what we pay attention to and what we pay attention to in life is limited to how our brains have been conditioned in our beliefs and biases. The reason for this is because your brain is bombarded with thousands of stimuli from your external environment, as well as your internal environment, which is your body, during every minute of the day. If you tried to pay attention to every single stimulus, you would literally go insane. To help you function in your world, your brain has been trained to only pay attention to what your brain thinks is relevant and everything else is filtered out. In your average workday, there are likely many things going around you that may be extremely important for you to know. Unfortunately, the way your brain was designed and how it has been conditioned since you were a child, prohibits you from seeing many of those situations. Every blind spot in your organization or team opens the door for multiple inactions on your part.

Some blind spots in your organization could be inequality of pay within your staff where men are paid more than women, or one of your managers behaving disrespectfully toward certain team members and so on. One of the greatest challenges for you as a leader is that you are always responsible for everything that goes on in their organization or team, even if you have no visibility.

In my experience, whenever I work with a leader who has been passed over for a promotion, it's not because of the big actions or big decisions to not act, it's generally because of the habitually small actions or inactions due to a lack of visibility that have slowly been eroding away at the leader's capacity to inspire trust in his or her people.

What's important to note here is that your daily actions and inactions are fuelled by the state of your mind and body that are working in harmony to dictate how you show up and act during every single minute of the day. None of these categories work as singular units. Your body is not separate from your mind, and your actions are never only mental or physical. They all work in symphony to dictate how you function and show up. What this means is that your mind, such as your thoughts, feelings, beliefs, biases, mood and so on, combined with your body, such as your posture, your vitality, and your body-language, all work together to dictate how you show up in your actions or inactions every single day, even when you have no visibility over them.

All of these factors, your body, mind, and actions/inactions in combination will prescribe what type of energy you are projecting at any given moment of the day and that type of energy will be felt by everyone in your environment.

In the following chapters, we're going to take a look at the different energies, how these energies show up in body, mind, and action, and which energies serve you best in which situations.

As we delve deeper into each of the energies, I will be sharing a number of scenarios showing examples of how these energies might show up in different situations. I have purposely written each scenario with a different flavour, in a different style, and I used a different energy while writing each of the scenarios. Some of these scenarios and styles of writing may resonate more with you than others. That's fine. That is the intention of the exercise.

While reading these scenarios, I invite you to not read the scenarios as if they are just stories, but to actually observe yourself in body, mind, and action while you are reading the scenarios, just like we practiced earlier in this chapter.

Practicing self-observation while you are observing the world and other people is in itself a powerful exercise that will help you identify how you are generating and projecting energy in different situations. Reading the following chapters while practicing self-observation will prepare you for when you start working on consciously shifting your own energy later on this book.

Chapter 8

Determined Energy

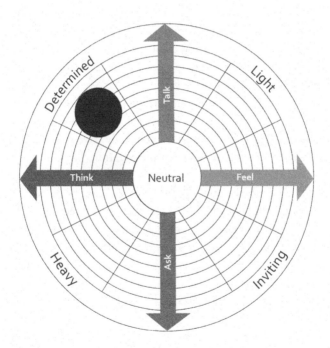

Scenario One

Imagine coming to work on a Monday morning after a nice relaxing weekend. You pass through the reception area, down the hallway, towards your office. Before you can get to your office, your boss's assistant comes hurrying down the hallway, telling you that your boss needs to speak with you urgently before you settle in for work. As she is hurrying down the hallway, you observe her body-language as she is leaning into the speed of her walk. Her facial expressions are showing signs of tension. Her body is contracted. Her gait is fast, deliberate, and lacks any bounce whatsoever. As she gets closer, you observe that her facial expressions look serious.

Your first thought, as she approaches you is: 'Oh-oh, my day is about to take a turn for the worse.' As she gets to where you are standing, she asks you politely, but urgently, to come with her to your boss's office as he needs to speak with you immediately. She then turns around and leads the way, as if she is expecting you to follow. You naturally follow and find yourself trying to keep pace with her, while she hurries back to your boss' office. While you are following her, you have a thousand thoughts going through your head, wondering what's happening. 'What did I do wrong now?' you ask yourself. 'It can't be the presentation I prepared on Friday, can it? My boss signed off on it already. Oh no! I bet something changed and I need to redesign the whole thing. I'm telling you, this boss has no clue how much time it takes to prepare these presentations. I already have so much work to do today. If he asks me to redo that presentation, I'm going to have a stroke.' And the thoughts just keep going on in your mind.

While all of these thoughts are going on, you begin to feel your body tense up. Your body begins to feel heavier. You feel your shoulders begin to tighten and crawl up toward your ears. Your focus is strictly on following your boss' assistant. You lose all peripheral vision. While you're following your boss' assistant, you pass your good friend and colleague, Veronica, who just got back from maternity leave. 'Hey,' she says, 'how are things?' Your own mind is racing at a 1,000 miles an hour at this point, and all you can utter to her in passing is, 'Gotta see the boss, catch up later?' You finally get to your boss's office and you notice how your energy has completely changed during that short walk from the reception to your boss's office. You were in such a good and relaxed place when you got to work, and within five minutes, your boss totally ruined it for you.

On reaching the office, your boss's assistant ushers you in to see him, and closes the door behind you. In a complete state of mental and physical activation, you find yourself being fully switched on and prepared for any disaster. Your boss, who is sitting behind the desk, just gets off the phone and looks up at you. 'Hey, how's it going?' he asks casually. You, in complete disaster mode answer using one word, 'Fine, what's up?' Your boss leans back in his big, leather, office chair, looks up at you and smiles. 'I just wanted to thank you for the great work you did on that presentation last week. It really made an impression on me and I promised myself that the first thing you hear on Monday morning is that I think you did a great job. So I told Mary to get you in here the moment you arrive this morning.' You stand there staring at your boss in disbelief thinking, 'Is that it?' But, of course, you don't tell him that. Instead, you reply to him politely, 'Well, thanks. Happy to help.' You make a 180-degree turn and head back to your office, still having a hard time processing what just happened. You can't shrug the tightness and heaviness you are feeling in your body and your mind is still racing at a 1,000 miles per hour.

You head back to your office and you find you just can't shrug that tightness and heaviness in your body. You decide to just get to work. Throughout your day, you notice that you don't feel like interacting with anyone and just want to get your work done, so you can go home. By the end of the day, you remember that you promised Mary you would check in with her. On your way out, you swing by her office, but she has gone home already.

That evening, you find it difficult to settle down and just have fun with your family. The heaviness that you experienced this morning is still with you and that is affecting your ability to just have fun. You find your mind constantly wondering back to work and it is making you feel exhausted and irritable. You decide to just turn in early and hope that tomorrow will turn out differently.

This scenario, as it played out, is a real life example of how energy projection, even with the best intentions, can have a negative impact on a person. First off, let's start with the boss. In this scenario, the boss projected Determined Energy, that had a good intention, to his assistant.

His enthusiasm to speak to you about your presentation drove the Determined Energy in him. However, his Determined Energy, no matter how positive the intention, was interpreted by his assistant as extremely urgent and important. The assistant also projected Determined Energy in the way she came to get you in the morning, but her sense of urgency created a negative perception in you. Her Determined Energy to get you into the boss's office as quickly as possible caused your energy levels to plummet from a place of Light Energy, where you were enjoying the aftereffects of a great weekend, to a place of Heavy Energy, where you were worrying about what you might have done wrong or what might be the problem.

Once you were stuck in that space, it became difficult for you to lift yourself out of that Heavy Energy, so you stayed in that space and just focused on getting your work done. In your Heavy Energy, you had no desire to socialize or even catch up with Mary. You also found it difficult to reconnect with your loved ones at home. This Heavy Energy state you found yourself in was also utterly exhausting for you, setting you up for a rough start to the week, despite having a really nice weekend.

What we can learn from this is that the energy you project doesn't necessarily mean it will be received as the same energy by the people you interact with. As a leader, being aware of the way you are projecting energy is only one part of the equation. It's also important to understand how that energy is being received by your people and how that is impacting the energy between your team members. Furthermore, in this scenario, you can see how Determined Energy can either occur as something positive, such as your boss' enthusiasm, or as something negative, his assistant's sense of urgency. What this means is that there are situations in your life and career where applying Determined Energy could serve you extremely well, but on the flip side, there are also situations where Determined Energy might not serve you so well.

When projecting Determined Energy might serve you well

As you could see in the previous scenario, Determined Energy is forward, or outward moving, and is generally activating. In any situation where you project Determined Energy, you are able to drive initiatives, mobilize people quickly, and get things done. When you project Determined Energy, you will tend to be concise in your way of communicating and setting boundaries with others is easier for you. Because of the forward driving nature of Determined Energy, you will be able to thrive in a competitive environment, and it will enable you to dominate in certain situations so you can exert autonomy and knowledge onto others.

Three values of projecting Determined Energy:

1. You thrive in the face of challenges
   When facing challenges, projecting Determined Energy helps you rise to the occasion. Determined Energy enables you to focus on, and control, outcomes. In this posture, you find yourself more able to be more inquisitive and be more independent. You're more comfortable opposing other points of views and expressing your own point of view with conviction. You are able to set clear boundaries in your relationships in work and in life.

2. You produce results
   When achieving results and outcomes is a priority, Determined Energy is essential. You are more able to focus to get things done and achieve the necessary results to get where you need to go. Using Determined Energy, you are so driven that you constantly look for new challenges and opportunities. You strive for success, and become even more energized and motivated when you run into obstacles.

3. When action is required, you are in your element
   Projecting Determined Energy helps you focus on achieving your goals quickly and forcefully. In this mode, you are quick to the point and rapidly shift your focus to what needs to be done, so you can continue moving forward. Moving onward and forward is your comfort zone and many of your successes in your life come from

your ability to quickly step into that Determined Energy, so that you can get the job done.

When projecting Determined Energy might not serve you so well

One downside of projecting Determined Energy all the time is that it is exhausting! Projecting yourself in a determined way to get people and projects moving requires a lot of energy and that energy is not always positive. Spending too much time in Determined Energy can result in burn-out in some people, and for many people, it can feel difficult to move out of that space, even in a social setting or with the people you love.

Another problem with projecting Determined Energy is that people in your environment don't always appreciate a person who projects Determined Energy all the time. Just like we saw in the earlier scenario, when you project Determined Energy, it can be interpreted by others as being aggressive, forceful, and could even be met with distrust. This, in return, may result in people not wanting to work with you as much or wanting to be around you.

Three challenges while projecting Determined Energy:

1. You may be viewed as being unsupportive.

    In situations that require an energy other than Determined Energy, you may find yourself feeling like a fish out of water. For example, your patience might be challenged in times where your team members just need you to listen, resulting in you becoming tempted to just 'give advice' or 'give your opinions' so that they can move on. This direct approach to 'helping' your team, even though you have the best intentions, could be interpreted by them as you being insensitive to how they are feeling, and what they are thinking.

    Over time, your team members may stop coming to you to brainstorm ideas, and with that, also stop coming to you with valuable feedback. Ultimately, this could result in a breakdown of communication and trust.

2. Projecting Determined Energy can be lonely.

Determined energy may serve us well when doing individual tasks, but in times of collaboration, projecting Determined Energy can be interpreted by others as being intimidating, aggressive, and overwhelming. Your ability to quickly come up with solutions and move rapidly into action may be very challenging for people who feel more comfortable in a more stable setting.

Your suggestions and ideas could be met with a great deal of resistance by people who need more stability and need time to weigh all the options, so that they can feel more confident in taking steps forward. Because you are so result- and solution-focused while projecting Determined Energy, people might begin to exclude you from brainstorming meetings and conversations. You may find yourself becoming isolated as more and more people begin to exclude you from their ongoing conversations.

3. Your Determined Energy could rock the boat a bit too much.

Some people tend to crave stability and certainty. They often focus on maintaining a predictable, orderly environment at work. People who like stability tend to be more cautious. They're likely to be more methodical and prefer to avoid rapid change where possible. For you, while in Determined Energy, stability could be interpreted as being 'boring', and may possibly make you a little impatient. Your Determined Energy may cause discomfort to those people who crave stability. They may begin to perceive you as someone who makes life difficult for them a bit too often. In situations like this, they may have the tendency to shy away from you when you project that Determined Energy.

Determined Energy in body-mind-action

As I mentioned earlier, Determined Energy is characterized by forward driving action. So, what does that look like in body, in mind, and in action? Below are some statements that represent Determined Energy.

1. I can be quite assertive when I need to be.
2. I come alive in a competitive setting.
3. When I think I am right, I become adamant and outspoken about my opinion.
4. I love to drive initiatives and ideas.
5. I love challenges and I'm not afraid to take a risk.
6. My muscles become tight.
7. My jawline tightens.
8. I lean into the situation.
9. My speech become short, concise, and to the point.
10. My vision narrows to focus on the issue at hand.

Now that you are aware of how Determined Energy might show up for you, I'd like you to spend some time observing yourself at work and in other aspects of your life to see how often, and in what type of situations, you find yourself projecting Determined Energy. Below is a scenario of what it could look like to consciously observe yourself in Determined Energy.

Scenario Two

It's Monday morning and it's the first day in your new role after your promotion. As the alarm goes off at 5 a.m., you find yourself thinking back about the interview process. In that interview process, your interviewer shared with you some critical feedback that she received from your previous manager. One thing that stood out for you was the feedback that your manager felt that you don't speak up enough during meetings and your manager feels that not speaking up during meetings might be an inhibiting factor in your new role. Despite that feedback, you still got the promotion, but the awareness that you are perceived as someone who doesn't speak up enough doesn't sit well with you.

Speaking up is not something that is in your nature. You prefer to see yourself as an observer and listener more than as a driver and talker. You know that in your new role, you are going to need to make some changes if you want to live up to the expectations.

You decide that you're going to do your best to be more of a driver in your new role. In that commitment, you decide to start your days in a more activated mode rather than in a passive mode, so you jump straight out of bed and get dressed to start your first morning run as a different type of leader. Even though your mind is trying hard to negotiate with you to go back to bed, you decide to override that inner voice, and start visualizing yourself as a strong and powerful runner, enjoying their run as the sun rises.

You manage to override that inner negotiating voice and head out the door to start your run. During your run, you find yourself already feeling so much accomplished and you can feel that driving energy within you, as you push yourself hard on your run. As you get back home from your run, you feel amazing and hold on to that energy as you shower, get changed, and get ready for work.

Once you arrive at work, you feel yourself walking to your office with focus and purpose. The first meeting in your calendar is with your new team. All of the team members were previously your colleagues, and one of those colleagues was passed over for the same promotion that you received. You realize that it will be important to set the tone with this team and to set some new boundaries with this team that you may not have done in the past while you were working with them. Five minutes before the meeting, you take a few deep breaths and reconnect with the amazing energy you were feeling on your run. While you're sitting behind your desk, you dig deep to start generating that same feeling in your body and mind and before you know it, you begin to feel strong and powerful. Your body feels tense but ready, like an athlete just before the start of a race.

As your team arrive one by one, you hold on to that energy you are feeling, and right away, your team notices that there's something different about you. You determined gaze, your upright posture, and the conciseness in your way of speaking all show someone determined to get the job done. Even your colleague who was passed over for your role notices that there's something different about you. During the meeting, he does try a few times to challenge you by being a bit abrasive in expressing his opinions. In the past, you would have let that slide, let him take control of the conversation, and just listen to him; but now, you respond quickly, concisely, and confidently. You notice how he is shifting in his chair trying to figure out what to do about this new version of you and you use that opportunity to push ahead with your agenda.

By the end of the meeting, you feel good because you have used your Determined Energy to set boundaries with your new team and feel you have succeeded in setting a new tone that this team is dealing with a different version of you who is not afraid to set a direction and handle confrontation where needed.

What makes this scenario very different from the first scenario in this chapter is that in the first scenario, Determined Energy was projected, but it was done unconsciously. In the second scenario, you consciously activated your Determined Energy to help you project yourself in a way that was of service to you. Of course, we could have lots of fun conversations about whether this was the best approach, but what is important at this stage of practice is to understand the difference between conscious and unconscious energy projection, so you can ask yourself whether the energy you are projecting is serving you at that specific moment.

Practice generating Determined Energy

Much like in tai chi chuan and qigong, we can use physical movements to practice generating energy in a certain way. Because Determined Energy is characterized by forward movement, we can simulate that forward movement in mind-body-action.

If you are sitting, I want you to sit up straight in your chair. If you are standing, stand with your feet apart at about hip-width. As you breathe, I want you to breathe in through your nose and out through your mouth. With every breath in, I want you to fill your lungs and stomach with as much air as you can. When you exhale, purse your lips, and force the air out of your lungs. The louder the sound of your exhalation, the better.

Now, when you inhale, I want you to draw your hands up to your chest, with your palms facing forward. In your next exhalation, forcefully push your hands out in front of you, until your arms are locked at the elbows. While you are extending your arms forward, imagine pushing hard against a heavy object or person. As you push away, feel yourself successfully pushing the object or person far away from you with one forceful push. Inhale and draw your hands back to your chest and repeat, like you are doing push-ups in the air.

While you are practicing this, your next challenge is to incorporate your facial muscles into the action. Recent research using functional MRI has shown that when we manipulate our facial muscles to mimic certain expressions, such as joy, anger, fear, and so on, the motion processing areas in the brain light up. What this means is that facial muscles don't only show a representation of how we might be feeling emotionally, but that this mechanism works in the reverse as well. By faking a smile, or by faking the expression of joy, we can fool the emotional centres of the brain to actually feel more happiness and joy.

So, what is the facial expression of determination? Well, think of a weightlifter who is lifting an extremely heavy weight. What facial expressions come to mind when you need to lift something very heavy? Your jaw locks, you show your teeth, the muscles in your throat tighten, and your eyes squint, as all of the muscles in your face contract.

So, now I want you to combine the body movement of that forward push and breathing technique with the facial expressions; do this ten times, using an imaginary resistance that makes you having to push extremely hard.

After your ten repetitions, try to relax and observe how the energy in your body and mind have changed from before you started.

One final tip, I recommend practicing this somewhere private. Doing this in public or around your family will earn you some interesting looks from people. I recommend locking yourself in the toilet or just finding a spot that is quiet and practice.

Wellness concerns when using too much Determined Energy

As I had mentioned earlier, Determined Energy is characterized by being forward moving or forward thinking, which requires the body and mind to be in a continuous activated state. When spending too much time in forward moving state, you may find yourself in a position where your body and mind become so accustomed to being activated that shifting gear and slowing down might become difficult for you. The ability to deactivate is a requirement for recovery. Without recovery, you run the risk of burning out at some point. Some points to consider when projecting Determined Energy for too long are:

1. Constantly driving forward can become exhausting.
2. Determined Energy could promote being too future focused, which can cause anxiety.
3. Driving initiatives can become stressful for yourself and for your people.
4. Determined Energy can reduce patience and promote frustration when things don't go as planned.
5. Incompetence in others can make you feel angry.
6. Making time for self-care may seem impossible.
7. Slowing down may become difficult.
8. Uncontrolled Determined Energy may interfere with sleep quality.
9. You may find that you take yourself way too seriously.
10. You may find yourself feeling lonely because the pushing factor may push people away.

By now, I hope you are noticing that as a leader or a boss, using only Determined Energy will serve you extremely well in some situations, but may not serve you well in many others. As a determined boss or leader, what situations can you think of where you showed up with Determined Energy, but did not get the outcomes you wanted? As a determined boss, or leader, how many people in your immediate circle may do better with a different energy from you?

As you move into the next chapters, I recommend observing yourself throughout your day and try to identify in which situations you show up with Determined Energy. Remember, we exhibit all the energies throughout the day, but tend to have one or two dominant ones. Observing yourself in your dominant energy mode will help you evaluate for yourself whether that is the energy that is serving you best.

Chapter 9

Inviting Energy

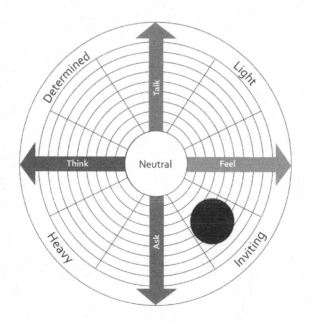

Scenario One

Joanne runs an international events team for a global non-profit organization. Being part of a non-profit organization means that many of this team's events are designed to raise money for the organization. Due to the COVID pandemic, the team was forced to shift to a virtual fund-raising format, rather than live events. To better manage the shift to a virtual offering, Joanne decides that the team would benefit from having someone on the team with more digital experience. After an exhaustive search, she finds a highly experienced consultant with over twenty years of experience in this space. Joanne feels this team will really benefit from the expertise and the wisdom this consultant will bring to the table.

A few short weeks in her new role, during the weekly virtual team huddle, the consultant begins to complain to Joanne and the team that she feels everyone is dumping their workloads on her and she is feeling overwhelmed. Knowing that the meeting has a lot of agenda points to cover, Joanne responds abruptly to the consultant by giving her advice on how she can better manage her workload, and then goes back to the meeting agenda. A few weeks later, the same thing happens again, and the consultant speaks up more angrily about how overwhelmed she is. Again, Joanne listens briefly to the consultant's concerns, then tells the consultant that she understands how the consultant is feeling, but that these are very challenging times, and everybody is overwhelmed. Joanne went on to tell the consultant that it's just the way things are right now, and Joanne's hands are tied. She then turns her attention to the team and tells the team to put more effort in supporting each other and the consultant.

A few weeks later, the consultant resigns, and in her resignation letter, she points out to Joanne that she never felt listened to. Upon reading that letter, Joanne responds with, 'What does she mean by saying she was not feeling listened to? I've had to listen to her complain since the day she arrived, and it didn't get us anywhere.'

In this scenario, what might be Joanne's energy projection? She is very forward focused; she is concise in her communication, and has a tendency to speak rather than listen. Even though Joanne felt that she was listening to the consultant, she wasn't listening to the consultant in a way that the consultant needed. The energy that Joanne was projecting in this scenario was of course Determined Energy. However, the type of energy that the consultant was needing was different from Determined Energy. In this scenario, the consultant would have benefitted from a leader who was projecting a more open and empathetic posture. What the consultant likely needed in this scenario was a leader who was able to project Inviting Energy.

Inviting Energy is the opposite of Determined Energy. Where projecting Determined Energy is about moving forward, projecting Inviting Energy is about drawing energy in. This is the energy of empathy, compassion, and understanding. Where Determined Energy is more about speaking up or speaking out, Inviting Energy is about asking questions and practicing listening that is genuine and caring. Just like with Determined Energy, there are situations where projecting Inviting Energy can serve you extremely well. However, there are also situations where projecting Inviting Energy might not serve you so well.

Where projecting Inviting Energy might serve you well

When you project Inviting Energy, you are in an open mood. You are the diplomatic team member who is known as a good listener and who can find understanding in other people's points of view, even if you disagree with them. People like to come to you with their problems and you genuinely care about how they feel. In times of dramatic change, you are likely the person who will be asked to initiate a change-management strategy, because you are known to be the person whom leadership can count on to take on this new challenge, and lead the initiative with empathy.

Three values of projecting Inviting Energy

1. People can count on you for support.
   When projecting Inviting Energy, it is easy for you to feel empathy for the people in your life. People feel like they can come to you with their problems and ideas because you are genuinely interested in what they are thinking and feeling. Caring is your ally while projecting Inviting Energy, and you're able to help people through challenges in a caring manner. Furthermore, you are open in your demeanour, and are receptive to the input from others, even when their opinions differ from yours.

2. You bring stability to the conversation.
   In times of change or crisis, you tend to be approached as the person to lead change or crisis initiatives because you bring a sense

of calmness and stability to the conversation. Your Inviting Energy has a deescalating effect on people, which brings a much needed sense of stability to the team. While projecting Inviting Energy, you are more capable of seeing solutions to problems that others might miss, making you a valuable asset.

3. You are a master collaborator.
    Inviting Energy helps you prioritize and strengthen relationships over tasks. People enjoy spending time with you because you are so caring and empathetic. Your caring energy makes it easy for you to pull teams of people together to collaborate on projects. Finally, because people enjoy including you in their projects, you will receive a lot of opportunities to get involved in other projects that increase your visibility within in the organization.

Where projecting Inviting Energy might not serve you so well

Projecting Inviting Energy all the time can be challenging because you run the risk of becoming everyone's doormat. Saying 'No' can be a challenge for you because you feel bad for people who have a problem, you want to be supportive, and help them through their challenges. Unfortunately, there are a lot of people with challenges and, sometimes, taking on too many responsibilities can leave you feeling utterly exhausted by the end of the day. Being too open and inviting can be a challenge if you are stuck with that Inviting Energy all the time. A lack of assertiveness, while being too agreeable, could mean that you end up having too much on your plate. This, in return, could result in a less than satisfactory quality of work and could even reduce your ability to meet deadlines altogether, resulting in a reduction of trust in the people you work with.

Three challenges while projecting Inviting Energy:

1. You may be viewed as being too passive.

In situations that require a different energy from Inviting Energy, you may find yourself feeling like a fish out of water. For example, in times of action where people turn to you for decisive and assertive leadership, your Inviting Energy may be interpreted as not being assertive enough. Over time, your team members may stop looking to you for direction, which could result in a breakdown of communication and trust.

2.   You struggle to say 'no'.
Being in an inviting posture may serve you well when supporting others but being too supportive means that you end up with a lot of work on your plate. Saying 'no' is difficult for you, and after a while, people learn to come to you to offload everything. With too much on your plate, you sacrifice your self-care time to take care of others, resulting in high levels of fatigue and potential burn-out. With too much on your plate and not enough time, the quality of your work drops, and you risk missing critical deadlines, which in turn may result in diminishing trust from your team and stakeholders.

3.   You struggle with having tough conversations.
People who have a tendency to be challenging in nature and are assertive in their opinions may make you feel uncomfortable when you project Inviting Energy. Your tendency to self-reflect and be thoughtful during conflict may make you appear as if you are not standing up for what you believe in, or standing up for the people you work with. Your Inviting Energy in these situations may make it difficult for you to engage in a tough conversation, and you may find yourself shying away from it, or shutting down. This, in turn, may be interpreted as a sign of weakness by your team members.

Inviting Energy in body-mind-action

Inviting Energy is characterized by drawing energy using empathy, compassion, and deep listening. So, what does that look like in body, in mind, and in action? Below are some statements that represent Inviting Energy.

1.   In my relationships with people, I tend to be very loyal.
2.   People in my team see me as being very helpful.

3. I open myself up to the ideas of others, even if they are different from mine.

4. People know me as being patient.

5. My leadership style is known to be collaborative.

6. My posture becomes open.

7. My heart feels warm.

8. I lean in attentively when others are speaking.

9. I can feel what other people are feeling.

10. I can see the bigger picture.

Scenario Two

After the early departure of the consultant, Joanne reflected hard on the events that led up to the resignation. Joanne decided to engage the services of a coach to help figure out what she could have done differently in this case.

Joanne learned about the different energies and came to the realization that her natural tendency is to project Determined Energy. Intrigued by this, Joanne wanted to explore what she could do to improve her Inviting Energy with her remaining team members. She decided to approach each team member to ask them for genuine feedback on her natural demeanour, to ask them for advice on what Inviting Energy would look like to them, and whether or not Inviting Energy would improve their working relationship. While considering asking for feedback, Joanne expressed concern that, in the past, she usually just received generic and positive feedback from her team, with not a lot of constructive input. While working with her coach, Joanne began to wonder if she wasn't receiving constructive feedback because she would be projecting Determined Energy while asking for feedback, which could be pushing people away from feeling comfortable about giving honest feedback.

She decided to practice generating Inviting Energy with her coach while also working on her deep listening skills. Over time, and with practice, Joanne began to notice that she was starting to talk less in meetings, and found herself asking more questions. She then noticed how her team members started coming to her with more input and suggestions on projects.

When she felt more confident in her practice of projecting Inviting Energy, Joanne approached each of her team members and asked them for honest feedback about how they observed her while in her natural determined state. She was shocked to hear that many of her team members really appreciated her ability to set direction and take tough decisions, but her determined demeanour could also be intimidating sometimes, making it challenging to share ideas, insights, and feedback with her, since she was their boss. This feedback was incredibly valuable to Joanne. She felt that with this new feedback, an opportunity for growth had opened up for her, and she was going to take that opportunity to be a better leader for herself, her current team, and any new staff members in the future.

An important lesson for Joanne, in this scenario, is how being in a determined state can greatly reduce the capacity to see things that are going on in her team, and how by shifting her state to a more inviting one, she was more open to receiving input that came from outside the line of her vision. In addition to that, her energy projection in a determined state was highly effective when needing to take tough decisions, but could also be extremely intimidating for some of her team members, which resulted in their hesitation to be honest with her.

What we can learn from this is that for a leader, it's critical to be aware of what their natural energy projection is, where that energy projection might serve them well, and where it might not serve them well. Knowing how to voluntarily shift into a different energy state is, therefore, a critical leadership skill.

Practice generating Inviting Energy

Just like the physical movements we practiced to help us generate Determined Energy, there are also physical movements to practice generating Inviting Energy. Unlike the Determined Energy exercise that is designed to push energy forward, the Inviting Energy exercise is designed to help you draw energy in.

Just like with the Determined Energy exercise, you can practice this either sitting down or standing up. If you are sitting, I want you to sit up straight in your chair. If you are standing, stand with your feet apart, at about hip-width. To start, I want you to focus on your breath, breathing in through your nose and out through your mouth. With every breath in, I want you to fill your lungs and stomach with as much air as you can. When you exhale, relax your jaw, and just let the air flow out of your lungs without any effort.

Now, when you inhale, I want you to draw your arms and hands up like you are hugging a beach ball. Remember to completely relax your arms and hands as you raise them into the air. Think of your arms as the arms of a string puppet with strings attached to your wrists and elbows while they are being pulled into the air by the puppet master.

As you exhale, still with your arms completely relaxed, open your arms up as wide as possible exposing your heart and chest. While you are doing this, I want you to tilt your head back, look up at the sky and smile. Imagine yourself opening your arms to give someone you love dearly the warmest hug you can imagine.

Just like with Determined Energy, incorporating a facial expression is critical to help activate the emotional centres. So, what's the facial expression of being inviting? It's the facial expression of warmth, care, and love. As you tilt your head back and open up your arms, put a warm and loving smile on your face. While you do this, let out a long sigh and say, 'Aaahhhhh,' for the entire duration of your exhalation.

While you are doing this, practice opening your eyes as much as you can, and practice broadening your field of view. Try to clearly see not only what is on the ceiling or in the sky, directly within your field of vision, but try to expand your field of vision laterally, so that you can bring objects in your peripheral vision into focus as well.

While you do this exercise, I also want you to imagine drawing energy in from the earth, through your feet and up your body, an simultaneously drawing energy in from the air around you, through the top of your head and into your body.

As you inhale, bring your arms back in to hug the beach ball and bring your head back into a neutral position with your gaze straight ahead. While you do this, I want you to imagine releasing that wonderful energy you received from the earth and air, and let it flow out of you through your feet back into the earth, and through the crown of your head back into the air.

Just like with the Determined Energy exercise, I want you to repeat for ten times. While you are doing this movement, try to blend your energy with the energy of the earth and air with each repetition.

After ten repetitions, relax for a moment, and observe how the energy in your body and mind have changed from before you started. Take a moment to observe how this exercise feels in your body as you blend your energy with your environment. Also, observe how practicing making the sound and increasing the limit of your vision change how you feel.

Wellness concerns of Inviting Energy

Being in an inviting posture is characterized by being in an open and empathetic state, which requires the body and mind to be in a continuously receptive and reflective posture. When spending too much time in an open state, you may find yourself in a position where your body and mind become so accustomed to being receptive that creating forward momentum becomes difficult for you, such as doing something for yourself, or driving your own ideas. The ability to be assertive is a necessary requirement for recovery, and without recovery, you run the risk of burning out at some point. Some points to consider if you find yourself projecting Inviting Energy for too long are:

1. Putting other people first all the time can be exhausting.
2. Your needs tend to come last, after everyone else's.
3. Your inability to say no means that you end up with way too much work on your plate.
4. In Inviting Energy, you risk becoming everyone's doormat.
5. Listening to everybody else's problems means you rarely get to talk about how you feel.
6. Having time for self-care is rare.

7. You risk feeling overwhelmed.
8. You risk feeling fatigued constantly.
9. You stop feeling playful.
10. You receive little support from others, even though you feel you support everyone else.

As you can see, being in Inviting Energy can seem like the ideal leadership energy. However, there are plenty of situations where being inviting may not serve you or your people well.

Can you think of any situations where your Inviting Energy did not serve you or your people?

Now that you're more aware of Inviting Energy, take some time to observe yourself throughout your day, and see if you can recognize yourself with Inviting Energy. How much time do you spend using Inviting Energy? Are there any situation where applying Inviting Energy would be your best option, and are there any situation where you may have applied Inviting Energy and it did not serve you so well? Just like with Determined Energy, being more aware of when you project Inviting Energy will help you evaluate for yourself whether it is the most effective energy to be in. Later on, in this book, you will be learning how to consciously choose an energy that works best for you in any scenario. But, until then, simply observe yourself first.

Chapter 10

Light Energy

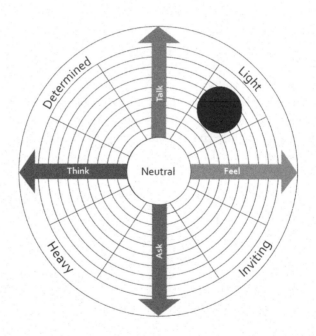

Scenario One

Justin is the regional CEO for the Pan-Asian division of a global IT company. Justin was generally known as a jovial leader, with a great sense of humour. He really felt that his carefree and personable demeanour was a major strength working for a company that thrived on innovation. He had great relationships with all of his country heads, and he really felt that his positive relationships with them was one of the major reasons why the Asian region had grown into a top earning sectors for this company.

Six months ago, things changed overnight as Justin received word from the global head office in Seattle that the company was being acquired by a global market leader, and that Justin needed to commence with preparing the region for significant changes ahead. However, before he could even commence with the preparations, the global head office made a public announcement that they were being acquired.

This sudden announcement left the Asian region in complete panic and turmoil. Almost overnight, Justin found himself in such a predicament that all he felt he was doing was putting out fires. He found himself going from one townhall meeting to another, trying to explain the acquisition to his people. An exhausting travel schedule, combined with the stress of managing uncertainty in his people, had a tremendous toll on Justin's energy.

As the days went by, Justin could feel his energy become increasingly heavier with every new policy announcement that would come from the new owner. As time went by, he could feel his natural sense of humour evaporate into thin air. He found it increasingly harder to project an uplifting image to his people. Furthermore, he started to receive resignation letters from his senior country heads as they were jumping ship, even though there was no mention that people would be losing their jobs. The feedback that he received was that the country leaders felt that the acquisition by this mammoth of an organization was likely going to bury the smaller innovative company with tons of corporate governance nonsense that was surely going to kill the entrepreneurial culture of his company. As his leaders started to leave, so did other talented players. Justin felt that the exodus of talent was going to be the death of him, and he found himself sinking deeper and deeper into a heaviness that was downright depressing. He could see his former self withering away, as he gradually lost all interest to take better care of himself. He hardly slept, lost any desire to exercise regularly, and found himself eating just junk food to fuel himself during his mega long days of putting out fires.

Justin knew that he had to turn things around, otherwise it would be the end of him, his career, and also the end of the company. He set up a strategy call with his entire leadership team with the hope of energizing the remaining leaders. In this call, Justin did his best to dig up as much energy as he could to try to push his team in activation mode. During the meeting, Justin did most of the talking, and found himself almost yelling at his team that the team had to come together as one, so that they could focus on getting through this time of change. Whatever concerns were raised by the team members, Justin found himself overriding the concerns and just telling them that this was not the time for self-pity; this was the time for action. After a short while, his team members stopped offering input, and instead, just started to agree with whatever Justin was proposing. After a whopping three-hour meeting, Justin was utterly exhausted, feeling like he was the one doing all the heavy lifting. On his way home that day, Justin was sitting in his car and started to feel emotional. Knowing that taking work home with him emotionally was not in his nature, he suspected that something was not right. He, then, reached out to his Human Resources Director and asked her to seek out a coach to help him get through the transition process.

The next day, I received a phone call from Justin's Human Resources Director, requesting a meeting with Justin. In my first meeting with Justin, he told me the whole story, and how he was starting to notice that he was no longer his former jovial self. We agreed that we would start working on Justin getting his positive energy back, and from there, help him find himself again, despite the chaos that he was in.

In this scenario, which is based on a number of true examples, what was Justin's natural way of projecting energy? He was a jovial guy and really valued the relationship that he had with his people. He was a people's person, first and foremost. On top of that, he was one of those people who naturally see the world through a positive lens, and he loved that about himself. However, as the circumstances changed, and with it the energy of the people around him, that negative energy began to rub off on him. Like a virus, that negative energy drove his energy down to a point where he wasn't able to recognize who he was anymore.

Losing all sight of himself in his involuntary state of heaviness was the catalyst for him to lose his effectiveness as a leader. As he saw himself moving ever further way from his natural self, he became increasingly more desperate. That desperation was felt by his team and they ended up shutting down as a result of his Heavy Energy. So, in this case, he was infected by the heaviness of the people around him and in return, fed that heaviness back to his people, creating a self-fulfilling prophecy of impending doom.

Just like with Determined Energy and Inviting Energy, there are pros and cons to each way we project energy. For someone who lives life where Light Energy is their default and unconscious way of energy projection, they tend to be strong in relationship building. Their positive, enthusiastic, and uplifting attitudes tend to make them very strong in their capacity to network and collaborate with others. However, as we can see in Justin's case, one challenge for people who by default project Light Energy is that they tend to draw their positive energy from their interactions with other people. Unfortunately, this also means is that they then run the risk of being affected easily when the energy of the people around them becomes anything other than light. One challenge for people who project Light Energy by default is to be able to consciously shift energy into any other state, without feeling like they are losing sight of their happy-go-lucky selves.

Where projecting Light Energy might serve you well

When you project Light Energy, you are in a flexible mood. You are able to get along with everyone and you can find humour in almost any situation. Being light helps you thrive in a competitive environment by building strong relationships and having a network of people who love to help you out where possible.

Your enthusiasm, especially in times of crisis, can be a powerful antidote for stress and anxiety in your team members. You become a beacon of hope and your ability to collaborate with anyone will open the door to opportunities that otherwise may never have been opened.

Three values of projecting Light Energy:

1. You bring enthusiasm to the table.

    When projecting Light Energy, it is easy for you to feel enthusiastic about new ideas and suggestions from others. Your upbeat nature makes it easy for you to communicate your ideas to others. Your high energy allows you to be positive, even in situations where others might not be. Humour is your ally while projecting Light Energy and you're able to overcome challenges in a lighthearted manner. Furthermore, you are flexible in your mood and are able to quickly pivot in a new direction when required, making you more adaptable.

2. You see an opportunity in every challenge.

    When presented with a challenge, you tend to approach those challenges with a sense of lightness that allows you to see a much bigger picture. Your ability to see larger concepts and bigger patterns in a state of lightness helps you identify solutions to problems that others might not see. While projecting Light Energy, you feel more confident taking risks, and you are less afraid of possible negative outcomes. Finally, your Light Energy enables you to learn from your mistakes, creating opportunities for growth in times of challenge.

3. You are a master networker.

    Projecting Light Energy helps you prioritize relationships over tasks. People enjoy spending time with you because you are carefree, funny, and spontaneous. Your Light Energy makes it easy for you to pull teams of people together to collaborate on projects. Finally, because people enjoy including you in their projects, you will receive a lot of opportunities to get involved in other projects, that increase your visibility in the organization.

Where projecting Light Energy may not serve you so well

Like we saw with Justin in the opening scenario, projecting Light Energy all the time can be challenging, because life is not always fun and games. Being too flexible and sociable in times of urgency can be a challenge if you are stuck in that light mood. A lack of urgency could mean that deadlines are not met, and promises are not kept. This, in turn, could reduce your co-workers' trust in you. People in your environment don't always appreciate a person who is projecting Light Energy all the time. Light Energy can be interpreted by others as being flaky and not able to take things seriously. This, in turn, may result in people not wanting to include you in some exciting project or consider you for more senior roles in your career.

Three challenges of being in a light posture:

1. You may be viewed as being out of touch with reality.

   In situations that require a different energy from being light, you may find yourself feeling like a fish out of water, which is what happened with Justin. For example, in times of crisis where people turn to you for leadership, your Light Energy may be interpreted as not being serious enough. Over time, your team members may stop coming to you for guidance or direction, which could result in a breakdown of communication and trust.

2. Urgency and speed are not your friends.

   Projecting Light Energy may serve you well when working with others, but during times that require the sleeves to be rolled up and to do some heavy lifting, you may find yourself struggling. Your Light Energy may prevent you from developing a pinpoint focus when required, making you susceptible to distractions. Your carefree nature may inhibit your ability to act with urgency in certain situations, putting you at risk of missing deadlines and breaking promises, which ultimately can result in resentment from others and a breakdown of trust.

3. You shy away from having tough conversations.

   People who have a tendency to crave stability and certainty often focus on maintaining a predictable, orderly environment, and will question people who operate outside of their comfort areas. Your carefree and lighthearted nature can be uncomfortable for people who crave more stability. You may find them pressing you hard in some situations. Projecting Light Energy in these situations may make it difficult for you to engage in a tough conversation, and you may find yourself shying away from it. This, in turn, may be interpreted as a sign of weakness by your team members.

Light Energy in body-mind-action

Light Energy is characterized by being in a carefree and optimistic state that is joyous, fun, creative, and which sees opportunities before challenges. Below are some statements that represent Light Energy in body, in mind, and in action:

1. I draw energy from being around people.
2. In a group setting, I tend to be the life of the party.
3. In team meetings, I find team harmony more important than pushing my opinions.
4. I see myself as being enthusiastic.
5. At work, I get excited about exploring new opportunities.
6. My posture feels taller.
7. I feel bouncy.
8. The tone of my voice sounds enthusiastic.
9. My face becomes more expressive.
10. I feel joyous.

Scenario Two

From his coaching, Justin came to the realization that even though his comfort zone was to be in Light Energy, always being in Light Energy was not serving him or his people well. Justin became aware that he needed to learn that voluntarily shifting himself into projecting other energies at appropriate times would serve him and his people much more.

Initially, Justin felt very uncomfortable with the other Energies as it didn't feel natural to him to project something that he was not accustomed to projecting. During our coaching sessions, I asked him which energy he thought he was projecting when he was questioning himself, while trying to practice projecting a different energy. As he practiced observing himself in mind-body-action, he noticed that questioning himself, while trying to learn a different way of projecting energy, was actually pushing him out of Light Energy. He noticed that instead of feeling light and energetic, his body would become tense. His breathing would become shallow and he could hear his own mind judging himself for being incompetent when it came to learning a new skill. I then asked him if this is how he saw himself in this merger. He thought about that for a moment and then looked me in the eye and smiled. 'That's exactly how I feel. I have never done anything like this before, and it's pushing me far out of my comfort zone. I have so many people counting on me, and I don't know if I am up to the task.' That was when Justin realized that he was simply responding to learning to do something new. With that realization, he remembered that whenever he learned a new skill in the past, he was always hard on himself until he felt like he had mastered the skill. Then, he felt like he could relax and be his happy-go-lucky self.

For Justin, this merger was a new learning opportunity. He was starting to realize that approaching this new learning experience while projecting Light Energy might serve him and his people more than approaching this new experience with his typical seriousness.

Justin asked me to shadow him for a few days and he let me observe him in real time in office and at meetings. This was a fantastic opportunity for me to see his mode of operation in real time. While interacting with others, I noticed how he would start off the meeting using Light Energy, making small talk, cracking jokes, and being joyful. However, the moment the energy from his colleagues would change to being more serious or sombre, his energy would shift into being more determined. At the end of the observation period, I shared with him my feedback and he mentioned how he was starting to notice how he was shifting his energy in these instances. We talked about the difference between unconscious and conscious energy projection and we explored what it would take for Justin to be more conscious about how he was showing up in his meetings.

Moving forward, Justin spent many hours practicing consciously shifting energy into different states in different situations, while also learning how to pull himself back into his beloved Light Energy after any voluntary shift of energy. In time, Justin became more confident shifting his energy and he noticed how the sense of self-control was really improving his sense of confidence.

A few months later, Justin had organized another team strategy meeting and asked me to join him to observe how he was doing. At the beginning of the meeting, the team was quiet and the weather in the room was gloomy. Justin walked into the meeting room and sat down at the head of the table. Looking at his team, he smiled. 'Can anyone tell me why we are meeting today?' he asked. 'We're here to work on a strategy,' said one of his team members. 'You're absolutely right,' said Justin. 'If we want to come up with some innovative ways as to how we can make things work in the future, we need to lighten the mood a little. Before we even start talking strategy, let's all lighten up the mood and have some fun. What do you all think about that?' Without waiting for an answer, Justin turned on the song 'I'm sexy and I know it' by LMFAO and started dancing. His team members all looked as if he had gone insane, but they were all smiling. Slowly, but surely, each of his team member got out of their chairs and joined him. After they were all done dancing, everyone sat down and Justin said, 'Just because we have a tough job to do, it doesn't mean we can't have fun while doing it.' Immediately, the energy in the room changed and everyone was smiling and nodding. Justin and the team went on to have one of the most productive meetings they have had in months. Justin did a great job of leading the team by bringing the team back into lightness after each healthy dose of seriousness. The team remained engaged and excited, and by the end of the meeting, they had come up with a ton of strategies regarding how to keep the company moving forward and making money, despite any new governance changes initiated through the acquisition.

After that day, Justin felt like he had got his mojo back. His confidence began to grow and with that, his energy, and his mood. By the time the acquisition was completed, Justin's team had managed to pull themselves together and they scored the highest grossing quarter the company had ever seen.

What we can learn from this is that there is a difference between conscious energy projection and unconscious energy projection. In Justin's case, the grief he was feeling when outside of his natural state of Light Energy was not necessarily because he found himself in another energy state that he did not like. Instead, his grief was likely being caused because he was feeling like a victim of the circumstances and did not have the tools to shift himself into a different state. By becoming more aware of the different ways he was projecting energy and by learning to become more comfortable being in different energy states, Justin started to learn that rather than seeing himself as a victim, he now had the power of choice to decide which type of energy he wanted to project in any situation. His power of choice shifted him naturally into a mood of possibility and exploration, which happens in a lightness, which is his comfort zone. With that sense of power came a renewed sense of confidence, which he then used to shift the energy in his team members as well. At the end of the day, it was Justin's courage to step out of his comfort zone, and practice projecting the different energies in body-mind-action until he became more comfortable in each energy state, that helped him overcome the overwhelming challenge he and his team were facing.

Practice generating Inviting Energy

Just like the physical movements we practiced to help us generate Determined Energy and Inviting Energy, we can do a similar movement to practice generating Light Energy. The objective of this exercise is not to push energy out or draw energy in as we saw with determined and inviting energies. The objective of Light Energy is to generate energy that helps us access joy, fun, curiosity, and wonder.

Just like with the other Energy exercises, this exercise can be practiced either sitting down, or standing up. If you are sitting, I want you to sit up straight in your chair. If you are standing, stand with your feet apart, at about hip-width. To start, I want you to focus on your breathing, breathing in through your nose and out through your mouth. With every breath in, I want you to fill your lungs and stomach with as much air as you can. When you exhale, relax your jaw, and just let the air flow out of your lungs without any effort.

Now, when you inhale, I want you to draw your arms and hands up to your shoulders. Remember to completely relax your arms and hands as you raise them into the air.

As you exhale, reach for the ceiling or the sky, leading with your palms, until you are completely stretched out. If you are standing, try to also straighten your legs and stand on your toes. Stretch yourself out as far as possible and feel the stretch from your palms down your arms, your spine, and into your hips. If you are standing, imagine that feeling travel all the way down to your toes, while you lengthen yourself as much as possible.

Just like with Determined Energy and Inviting Energy, incorporating a facial expression is critical for activating the emotional centres. The facial expression of Light Energy is that of immense joy and happiness.

As you stretch yourself, practice putting on the biggest smile possible. Your smile should be so large that it almost makes the muscles cramp around your mouth. Together with your grand smile, open your eyes as much as you can, and practice generating that joyous energy within yourself. While you are stretching yourself and exhaling, imagine the joyful energy building up within you and pouring out through the top of your head, like a fountain. Imagine yourself being showered with your joyful energy, as you are smiling that huge beautiful smile, with eyes wide open.

For each of us, the physical sensation of joy can be a completely different experience. Some of us might feel a tingling sensation through the body. Others might feel warmth. You might even feel itchy. You may even feel nothing at all. Especially, if this is a very unnatural exercise for you, you may not feel anything at all in the beginning. If that's the case, don't get frustrated. Just like with Justin, it takes time to practice projecting energy in states that are uncommon for you. Even if you feel nothing, just imagine yourself being showered by your own joy, happiness, and fun.

As you inhale, bring your arms down; and if you are standing, drop your heels back onto the ground.

Just like with the other energy exercises, I want you to repeat this ten times. While you are doing this movement, try to shower yourself with your joy, and try to expand the range of the fountain of joy you are creating around you, filling your environment, and the people in it with your Light Energy. Let them bathe in your joy and happiness.

After your ten repetitions, relax for a moment and observe how the energy in your body and mind have changed from before you started. Take a moment to observe how this exercise feels in your body as you shower your environment with your joyful energy.

Wellness concerns of Light Energy

Being in a light posture is characterized by being in a flexible, curious, playful, and joyful state which requires the body and mind to be in a continuously adaptable posture. Just like with the other energies, when spending too much time in a joyful state, you may find yourself in a position where your body and mind become so accustomed to being light that finding stability becomes difficult for you. The ability to feel centred, balanced, and stable is a necessary requirement for recovery. Without recovery, you run the risk of burning out at some point. Below are some challenges that you can encounter when you spend too much time being projecting Light Energy:

1. Being friendly all the time can be exhausting.
2. Being light may not benefit you in times where applying self-discipline is required.
3. A lack of self-discipline may result in missing deadlines, which can cause stress.
4. A lack of drive may result in frustration when not producing desired results.

5. Being joyful can be misinterpreted by others as not taking the job seriously.

6. A perceived lack of seriousness from others may result in being overlooked for promotions.

7. Being care-free may result in poor time-management.

8. Being joyful in high pressure environments may feel stressful or overwhelming.

9. Having a large social network can result in a social calendar that is more exhausting than work.

10. Your heavy social calendar may result in a lack of sleep or poor health habits.

In my experience, Light Energy seems to be interpreted by many leaders as an ideal energy. It may seem that using Light Energy is energizing, fun, and uplifting. This is not wrong. However, there are many situations in work and life that require a degree of assertiveness, seriousness, and discipline. Just like with the other energies, Light Energy will serve you extremely well in the right situations, but not in other scenarios.

How much time each day do you spend projecting Light Energy? If it's not that much, then perhaps practicing Light Energy could help you expand your repertoire. On the other hand, if you spend a lot of your time in Light Energy, are there situations where using Light Energy is getting in the way of your ability to be assertive, drive initiatives, and create more success as a leader or boss?

Observing yourself throughout the day will help you understand where your energy is serving you and where it is not.

Chapter 11

Heavy Energy

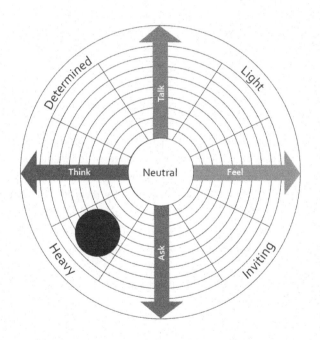

Scenario One

Recently, I was approached by a prospective client to help him work on overcoming some challenges that he felt were holding him back in his career. A twenty-year veteran of a global bank, Sandeep felt that even though he was only in his late forties, he had hit a ceiling in his career at the bank he was currently working at. Sandeep wanted to explore whether he should make a switch to another bank or research whether there is something in his way of operating that is preventing him from being promoted.

During our first meeting, Sandeep disclosed that he started his banking career working in the compliance department. When he was young, he really enjoyed the precision and consistency that was required in his role. At the time when he met me, Sandeep was in charge of a compliance department that employed over 100 people. When I asked him what he felt was the department's current happiness level, he honestly felt that the department was quite happy.

We then went on to explore Sandeep's mode of operation at work, at home, and in life. Sandeep described himself as an introvert who believed that the quality of work should speak for itself. He also considered himself a realist who felt very strongly about doing the right things in the right way. I then asked him about some aspects of his work that he didn't enjoy. His answer was immediate and firm. 'It's the politics. I severely dislike all the politics that comes with the job,' he said. When asking him what that meant to him, he explained that many of the meetings that took up his day were a waste of time, and about issues that could easily be resolved without him. If he didn't have to waste so much time and energy on those unnecessary meetings, he would get so much more work done in a day and would probably be much more productive. Sometimes, he felt that without those meetings, he would be able to showcase his abilities to the upper management by accomplishing so much more than he was doing now.

At the end of the meeting, I asked Sandeep if he would be willing to seek feedback from a number of his team and from upper management. Initially, Sandeep was a little hesitant to ask for feedback. His mindset was that people who give feedback don't fully know the situation he's in, so the feedback is never accurate anyway. Curious about that, I asked him what accurate feedback would look like in his case. He clarified that accurate feedback would be feedback that accurately describes him. I then asked him what kind of feedback he has gotten in the past.

His reply was that feedback had generally been inaccurate and that much of the feedback he received described him as reserved, fixed in his opinions, and not very personable. He then quickly went on to explain to me why he felt that the feedback was incorrect.

As a compromise, I asked him if he would be more comfortable asking for advice rather than feedback. I went on to explain that at times asking people for advice on how best to move forward can offer great insights into possible blind spots, while also offering suggestions on what can be done to overcome those blind spots. Sandeep agreed to speak to at least five people and ask for their input.

Two weeks later, we met up again, and Sandeep was very pleased with the advice he had received. Interestingly, almost all of the people recommended to Sandeep that he would be much more effective as a leader if he put more energy and time into building stronger relationships with the key people in the organization. At this point, even though he had the reputation of being a very solid performer, people felt that he was not making himself visible enough within the organization. According to the advice he had received, improving his visibility would greatly improve his chances of having an even more fruitful career at his bank.

Based on that information, we had a chat about his energy at work as it relates to the advice he had received. Sandeep came to the realization that his default way of overcoming challenges was by hunkering down and diving deep into his work, until the job was done. This realization was pivotal for Sandeep because, for the first time in his career, he was beginning to see how valuing his work duties over his relationships had brought him great success as an expert in his field, but his lack of relationships was holding him back.

Even though Sandeep is an alias of an actual client I once had, this is a very common scenario that I see with many executives. All too often, high performers rise through the ranks because they are producing tangible results for the organization. These tangible results are often produced by working hard and by acquiring exceptional expertise in a certain field. However, the higher they grow in their careers, the more relationship oriented their jobs become as they begin to take on larger, leadership-type functions. Many professionals are ultimately promoted to a point beyond their experience, knowledge, and capability, and must learn to leverage the relationships they have with their people, their managers, and many other people throughout the organization to continue producing results at a larger scale. In other words, they need to move from being the expert results-producer themselves to becoming an expert relationship-builder who can pull people together to produce results at a much greater level. For some professionals, this shift can feel quite natural, but for many others, like in Sandeep's case, this might leave them feeling like a fish out of water. For someone like Sandeep, learning when Heavy Energy serves them well and when it doesn't is critical in their evolution as a leader.

Where Heavy Energy might serve you well

When you project Heavy Energy, you are in an immovable mood. You are the realist team member who is able to offer a sense of reality to the conversation. While projecting Heavy Energy, you know what you are talking about. You are the specialist in the team who knows how to get from point A to point Z. Your work is meticulous, and you take great comfort in working in a field where you are the expert.

Three values of being in Heavy Energy:

1. People can count on your expertise.
    When projecting Heavy Energy, it is easy for you to tap into your breadth of knowledge. Your quiet demeanour lets you speak only when something is worth saying. And that means that when you do speak, people can count on you knowing what you are talking about. Your confidence in your knowledge inspires confidence in others, and when it comes to problem-solving, you are the go-to person.
2. You bring stability to the conversation.
    During times of change or crisis, people tend to turn to you for advice. Much more than your knowledge, you have the ability to dig deeper into the subject matter than anyone else. While projecting

Heavy Energy, you are strong in your beliefs about what is right and what is wrong; that can inspire a sense of stability and confidence in your team.

3. You get the job done, no matter what.

    Using Heavy Energy helps you prioritize doing the work necessary to produce results. You are not afraid to roll up the sleeves and get to work yourself. Nobody in your team is more dedicated to finishing the task and solving problems than you are. You are also a person of strong values and when you make a promise, you are committed to keeping that promise. Your ability to deliver results and dig deep into the subject matter makes you a valuable asset for any team.

Where having a heavy posture might not serve you so well

Projecting Heavy Energy all the time can be challenging because you run the risk of being seen as someone who looks at everything from a glass-half-empty perspective. One of the challenges that you can experience in this posture is that people don't like to include you in brainstorming sessions because they may perceive you as a bit of a buzzkill. On top of that, if you encounter someone who is extremely passionate about their point of view, you tend to shut down rather than speak up. This can result in becoming invisible and you may even find yourself being passed over for promotions by people who are junior to you.

Being too heavy and immovable in your area of knowledge can be a challenge if you are stuck in that mode all the time. A lack of perceived positivity, while not being assertive, could be perceived by others as being passive-aggressive and may result in people not wanting to include you in larger conversations.

Three challenges of being in a heavy posture:

1. You may be viewed as being too inflexible.

    In situations that require an energy different from Heavy Energy, you may find yourself feeling like a fish out of water. For example, while the team is brainstorming, you may find yourself often disagreeing with ideas because they don't seem practical, functional, or realistic. In these instances, your Heavy Energy may be interpreted as being inflexible. Over time, your team members may stop sharing new ideas with you, which could result in a breakdown of communication and trust.

2. You may struggle with change.
    Projecting Heavy Energy may serve you well in times of stability, but being too stable could mean that you struggle during times of disruption or if change is initiated by the leadership. Your Heavy Energy may predispose you to dig your heels into what you know best, and you may find yourself struggling with pivoting away from your comfort zone. Your hesitation in responding to change with enthusiasm may result in a lack of confidence from your stakeholders during dynamic times, and you may find yourself being left out of meetings regarding change initiatives.

3. You struggle with conflict.
    People who have a tendency to be confrontational and who are assertive in their opinions of you may make you feel uncomfortable. Your tendency to think about how to get the job done before you speak your mind can result in being misinterpreted by a confrontational person. They may perceive you as someone who shuts down during conflicts, rather than see you as the deep thinker that you are. Your silence could result in an escalation in energy from others who are impatient, leading to a possible breakdown in communication.

Heavy Energy in body-mind-action

The opposite of Light Energy, Heavy Energy is characterized by being in a grounded and righteous state that is stable, serious, disciplined, and tends to appreciate safety over opportunity. Below are some statements that represent Heavy Energy in body-mind-action:

1. I draw energy from completing tasks or solving problems.
2. In a group setting, I tend to be the observer.

3. In team meetings, I tend to have a sensible grasp of reality.
4. I see myself as being self-disciplined.
5. At work, I prefer to work on my own.
6. My posture becomes contracted.
7. My body feels like it's weighted down.
8. The tone of my voice becomes stable.
9. My jawline and shoulders become tight.
10. I want to feel safe.

Scenario Two

After Sandeep got the feedback, he became aware that spending too much time using Heavy Energy may be preventing him from building stronger relationships with key stakeholders in the organization. He mentioned that he would like to start practicing building relationships using his newfound awareness. In our session, I invited Sandeep to rehearse the different energies, just like I have shared in this book and he quickly realized that his body and mind felt most comfortable with the Heavy Energy and Determined Energy, but he felt much less comfortable when trying to project Light Energy and Inviting Energy. Deploying Inviting Energy and Light Energy felt extremely strange and uncomfortable to him. As we explored this further, it began to dawn on Sandeep that networking and relationship building require a great deal of lightness and that he might have been resisting the act of building relationships because it was too far out of his comfort zone.

Sandeep decided that this was something he really wanted to start practicing. Over the next few months, Sandeep would rehearse the different energies every morning, using the exercises in this book. Sandeep also pledged to do the Light Energy exercise before reaching out to the stakeholders in his company so that he would feel more relaxed and casual when communicating with them. After a few weeks, Sandeep began to notice that shifting into Light Energy was starting to feel less challenging. He also began to notice that he caught himself, on a number of occasions, smiling for no reason whatsoever.

When meeting with the stakeholders in his company, he would practice the Light Energy exercise before the meeting. During every meeting, he could notice that the people he met with would be smiling and appearing very relaxed with him. In those meetings, he found that his stakeholders would be extremely forthcoming with giving him feedback and tips, but more surprisingly, they would introduce him to other people in their respective networks.

One day, after a few months, Sandeep made an extremely bold move and decided to write an email to the global CEO of the company in New York. Not once, in his entire career, had he ever done something so ambitious. To his amazement, the global CEO was interested in speaking to him. During their phone conversation, the CEO mentioned to Sandeep that he had been hearing Sandeep's name quite a bit over the past few months and wanted to let Sandeep know that whatever he was doing differently, to keep doing it. He also gave Sandeep some extremely valuable advice on what he felt Sandeep should work harder at if he wanted to take his career further at the bank. Sandeep thanked him deeply and called me right away after the call.

The advice that Sandeep received from the CEO was that if Sandeep were to take on a bigger role at the bank, he would need to start showcasing his leadership skills more, so Sandeep's manager would have more confidence in placing him into a role that would put him in charge of a much larger group of people. Sandeep was so excited to hear this feedback that he now wanted to shift gears and start working on becoming an even more confident and competent leader.

When I asked him what it would take for him to become more competent and confident, he confidently answered that he needed to become more strategic at consciously applying the different energies. He realized that to receive input from others and build a support network, he needed to become even more comfortable being in Inviting and Light Energy. However, while taking the final decisions on what direction the team should be going, he also needed to practice being in Determined Energy, and then to be able to utilize his default energy of heaviness to complete tasks and see that projects are completed in a timely fashion.

An important insight for Sandeep in this scenario is that no one energy is better than the other. As a leader, Sandeep will need to become comfortable and well versed at applying all five energies. Projecting Heavy Energy has amazing benefits when we need to apply self-discipline, build strategies, and complete tasks. However, without mastering the other Energies, other critical skills like creating a vision, delegating effectively, collaborating with others, and seeking feedback may not be fully capitalized on. In many leaders today, I see this scenario play out time and time again. All too often, leaders are so caught up in the business of their day-to-day routines that they forget to scrutinize their own limitations as a manager or leader. Without that awareness, a leader or manager can't grow. Without personal growth, there is also not much chance of growth in your career.

Practice generating Heavy Energy

Just like the physical movements we practiced to help us generate the other energies, we can do a similar movement to practice generating Heavy Energy. The objective of this exercise is not to push energy out or draw energy in as we saw with determined and inviting energies, nor is it to help us access joy, fun, curiosity, and wonder, like when we practiced being in Light Energy. The objective of practicing Heavy Energy is to access the energy of self-discipline, stability, safety, and being grounded.

Just like with the other Energy exercises, this exercise can be practiced either sitting down, or standing up. If you are sitting, I want you to sit up straight in your chair. If you are standing, stand with your feet apart, at about hip-width. To start, I want you to focus on your breath, breathing in through your nose and out through your mouth. With every breath in, I want you to fill your lungs and stomach with as much air as you can. When you exhale, relax your jaw, and just let the air flow out of your lungs without any effort.

Now, when you inhale, I want you to move your hands up along your body to your shoulders. Remember to completely relax your arms and hands as you raise them in the air. Your palms should be facing up and your elbows should be bent so your hands are hovering in front of your chest.

As you exhale, rotate your palms toward the ground and press your hands down toward the ground with your thumbs staying close to your body. If you are standing, try to bend your knees and move your tailbone down, toward the ground, so you are in a squatting position. At the end of the movement, your arms should be completely straight, pointing down to the ground, and your palms should still be facing the ground. As you press down, round your shoulders forward and contract your stomach muscles, making them as firm as possible. If you are sitting, try to sink deeper into your chair while still rolling the shoulders forward, straightening the arms, and contracting your stomach muscles.

While you perform this exercise, I want you to imagine pushing your energy into the ground. Feel your energy flow from your body, down your legs, through your feet and travel down toward the centre of the earth. Think of yourself growing long roots of energy that project downward into the ground that give you stability in your stance.

Just like with the other energies, incorporating a facial expression is critical to activate the emotional centres. The facial expression of Heavy Energy is that of seriousness.

As you sink into the stance and push down with your hands, practice tightening your jaw and create a slight squint around your eyes. Together with your grounding posture, narrow your vision to see only what is right in front of you.

As you inhale, slide your hands back up along your body and rotate your palms to face up. Straighten out your posture by rolling your shoulders back and relaxing your stomach muscles. Relax your facial expression. While returning to the beginning of this movement, imagine drawing the roots back up from the ground and back into your body. As you pull your hands up, imagine reeling in the roots from the ground like you are reeling in a fish. Pull the roots back up into the body as you inhale.

Just like with the other energy exercises, I want you to repeat this ten times. While you are doing this movement, try to make yourself heavier with each repetition, while still being able to pull yourself out of heaviness between each repetition.

After your ten repetitions, relax for a moment and observe how the energy in your body and mind have changed compared to when you had started. Take a moment to observe how this exercise feels.

Wellness concerns of Heavy Energy

Projecting Heavy Energy is characterized by being in a stable and grounded state, which requires the body and mind to be in a continuously contracted and immovable posture. When spending too much time in a contracted state, you may find yourself in a position where your body and mind become so accustomed to being contracted that initiating a change in posture becomes difficult for you. The ability to be agile in both mind and body is a necessary requirement for recovery. Without recovery, you run the risk of burning out at some point.

Below are some challenges that you could encounter when you spend too much time projecting Heavy Energy:

1. Being heavy all the time can be exhausting.
2. Craving stability may result in stress and anxiety.
3. The need for knowing specific details may lead to frustration.
4. Seeing incompetence in others may cause stress.
5. Being too deeply involved with your team's work may result in a loss of visibility.
6. You may find yourself taking your career and your life way too seriously.
7. You may struggle to switch off at the end of the day.
8. You may feel lonely due to a lack of a support network.
9. Being playful, even with your kids at home, can become a challenge.
10. Your tendency to overthink and over-plan can cause chronic fatigue.

Applying Heavy Energy is critical if we want to apply self-discipline and hunker down to get work finished. Right now, as I'm writing this, I'm looking out of the window. The weather outside is absolutely gorgeous. As tempted as I am to close my laptop, go outside, and have fun, I am using my ability to harness my Heavy Energy to stay put and keep writing. Without my ability to access my Heavy Energy, even during moments when I don't feel like it, I don't think you would have been reading this book anytime soon.

For yourself, are there any unfinished tasks or projects out there that might benefit from some Heavy Energy so you can hunker down and get them finished? On the other hand, if you are someone like Sandeep, you may find yourself spending too much time deploying Heavy Energy. If this is the case, are there any situations in your life where that might not be serving you well?

Taking some time to observe yourself using Heavy Energy will help you determine where in your life Heavy Energy is the right Energy to use, and where accessing a different Energy might get you different results.

Chapter 12

Neutral Energy

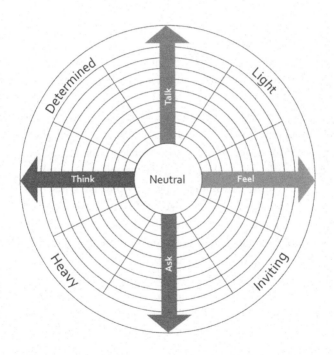

Scenario One

In the previous chapters, I had shared scenarios of clients in work settings. As compelling as those examples are, I do think it's important to mention that we don't only project energy at work. Oftentimes, the energy we project in our private lives can have a much greater impact on us. To shake things up, and to show that I too am only human, I would like to share a true story about something that actually happened to me in my personal life when I didn't manage my own energy effectively, in particular, when I found myself spending too much time in Neutral Energy.

Recently, my twenty-one-year-old daughter, Kilani, invited me to join her on a snowboarding trip. Fully appreciative of the fact that at twenty-one years of age, Kilani still enjoys the company of her old man, I jumped at the opportunity and said yes without hesitation. I could feel how being receptive to the invitation enabled me to feel a massive amount of Light Energy. The image of effortlessly going down the white, snow-covered mountain, with my daughter by my side, triggered immense joy and happiness.

However, shortly after committing to the trip, reality kicked in and I came to the realization that I hadn't been on a snowboard in over thirty years. With that realization, my mind automatically began to fill itself with all types of possible scenarios of how this could possibly end very badly for me. Instead of seeing myself gliding down the slopes with grace and joy, the scenario changed to something completely different as I saw myself fumbling, stumbling, flying, rolling, and sliding down the slopes, inviting all types of fractured limbs and a fractured ego. As that scenario played out in my mind, I could feel my body become extremely heavy, and with it, I could sense how my enthusiasm for the trip became overpowered by the sheer terror of possible injury and embarrassment.

Being aware that this was just a scenario playing out in my mind, I made a pact with myself to not let the Heavy Energy get in the way of the possibility of having an incredible experience with my daughter. Even though the uncertainty of how snowboarding would work out for me after thirty years was terrifying, I pledged to myself that I would not let it get in the way of my trip. The agreement that I made with myself was that every time I would feel myself becoming heavy while thinking about the trip, I would try to change my energy to that of Light Energy. To help me achieve that, I promised myself that I would double down on my meditation practice.

A few weeks later, it was time for our trip. I was extremely proud of myself for how I was able to meditate away the fears that I was feeling. After arriving at our destination, we had a very nice dinner together. Over dinner, Kilani seemed very happy and proud that her old dad was joining her on this trip. She even mentioned a few times how excited she was to be on the slopes with me the next day. Looking at her twenty-one-year-old face that was full of smiles, I couldn't help but be reminded of her when she was five years old, and super excited about going to the beach with her mom and dad. Even though she was twenty-one, I could still clearly see that five-year-old inside her and that sparked a tremendous warmth inside me. Unfortunately, the warmth and happiness that I was feeling was soon taken over by another bout of sheer terror. The realization hit me that I was less than twelve hours away from finding out whether or not I would still be able to carve the slopes, or if the slopes were going to be carving me, while I would be sliding down the slope, head first.

I decided that before going to sleep, I was going to practice some serious visualization and meditation to help keep my mind in a joyous and positive state. Thankfully, before going to bed, I happened to go through a very deep meditation session and came out of the session feeling extremely balanced and relaxed. I felt calm, centred, and ready for whatever the experience was going to be for me on the slopes.

After that deep meditation, I fell asleep quickly and had the deepest sleep I had had in a long time. Interestingly, I woke up about five hours later, in the middle of the night, wide awake. I woke up so extremely alert, I felt ready to go right then and there. Since it was 4.30 a.m. in the morning, that was not an option, given the slopes only opened at 8.30 a.m.. I really felt at that time that if I could just hold on to that balanced feeling until we hit the slopes, I would be fine, no matter what happened. I settled back into bed and decided to resume my meditation practice from the night before. Amazingly, I had another extremely deep and profound experience while in meditation and I managed to keep myself in deep meditation for hours. Needless to say, I felt incredible when arising out of my meditation and felt extremely confident going into the day.

After meeting up with Kilani in the lobby, we walked over to the ski lift, and all the while I felt a heightened sense of everything. I remember looking up at the sky. The sky was an incredible deep blue, with not a cloud in sight. The sun was already shining and I could feel the sunrays hit my face, as if I was being showered by warmth and love. Honestly, it felt like I was on drugs. I was so spacey that everything I encountered seemed extra amazing. Every person, every animal, every plant, and every snowflake left me in a state of awe. I was living in the moment and experiencing every moment with the most intense awareness, and I was loving it. I was so in the moment that I barely noticed that we had hopped on the chairlift. While the chairlift was carrying us to the top of the slope, I was in awe of the beauty around me. I noticed the beautiful white snow-covered mountain with an amazing blue backdrop that was the sky. It was like Kilani and I were floating inside an awe-inspiring painting.

While I was so deeply present in the experience, I failed to pay attention to the fact that the chairlift had arrived at the top of the slope. Now, if you ever see a snowboarder in a chairlift, you'll notice that snowboarders sit on the chairlift, their front foot attached to the binding and the rear foot out of the binding. The reason for this is so that the snowboarder can use the back leg to push themselves around while being on a flat surface. Only before they go down the slope will they attach the rear foot to the snowboard binding. When the chairlift reaches the top of the slope, it does not stop, but loops around and continues back down the slope. At the top of the slope, skiers and snowboarders slide out of their seats, on their skis and snowboards, gliding away from the lift while the lift loops around and heads back down the slope. Seeing skiers and snowboarders do this so gracefully is in itself inspiring. This is especially true for experienced snowboarders, who can glide gracefully out of the chairlift seat while balancing with only one foot in the binding.

When it was finally mine and Kilani's turn to glide out of the lift, I was all smiles and completely spaced out. I remember the moment my snowboard made contact with the snow and I was thinking to myself, 'This is so awesome.' Still smiling, I pushed myself away from the ski lift and at that moment, everything went south. After about one second of gliding, my snowboard took on a life of its own and decided to slide in a different direction than I wanted it to. Instead of sliding away from Kilani, my board slid right up against hers and we both ended up tumbling over each other, rolling away from the ski lift. In shear panic, the ski lift operator stopped the lift, so we wouldn't get hit by the lift chairs behind us. Once Kilani and I finally came to a stop, we both got up, looking back at the people on the ski lift behind us. With many annoyed and disappointing faces staring at us for holding up the lift, I made my best effort to find humour and pulled off a two-handed thumbs up, yelling, 'Sorry. My Fault. Old man on the ski lift.' As Kilani and I moved ourselves out of the way and the ski lift resumed operation, we were met with many endearing smiles as the people behind us resumed their graceful dismounts.

Kilani and I looked at each other, and after a quick 'Are you OK?' we headed to the top of the slope. While pushing myself over there with my back foot, I noticed that I was having difficulty stabilizing myself on my board. After three pushes with my back foot, , I again fell over. I realized that I was already fumbling and stumbling, even before hitting the slopes. Reaching the top of the slope, I fastened my back foot into the rear binding of my snowboard and said to myself, 'Well, here we go!' I pointed the front of the snowboard down the slope and just leaned forward, like I had remembered doing thirty years ago. The moment I gained momentum, I realized that I was still so spaced out that I had no stability whatsoever. On my first turn, I lost all sense of balance and just fell over backwards, landing on my back and sliding down the slope, headfirst, with my snowboard up in the air. In the distance, I could hear Kilani yelling, 'Daaaaad, are you OK?' I decided at that moment that it would probably just be best to let gravity do its work while I am on my back. I finally came to a stop where the slope flattened out a little. I decided to pick myself up and give it another try, which was met with the same fate. By the time I reached the bottom of the mountain, I had spent more time on my back than I had on my board. Battered and bruised, I looked back at the mountain and thought to myself, well, that's one for the mountain, and zero for me. As I stood there reflecting on what had just happened, I couldn't help but notice how spaced out I was before going up the mountain, and began to wonder what my snowboarding ability would have been like if I were projecting a different energy.

As I highlighted earlier in this book, mindfulness meditation can be an extremely powerful tool of self-care, self-management, and leadership. I also mentioned briefly how practicing mindfulness— the way of being present so as to prevent mindlessness—is quite different from practicing mindfulness meditation. With regards to preventing mindlessness, mindfulness meditation is not the only tool in the toolbox of a mindful and wise leader. As we can see in the real life example that I experienced recently, there are times where being meditative can serve us extremely well. However, just like with everything else in this universe, what might serve us well in certain situations, like where it helped me reduce my anxiety while anticipating hitting the slopes, it might not serve us well in others, like when I was too spacey to actually make it out of the ski lift, let alone be able to snowboard down the slopes. Where mindfulness meditation might serve us well is to quickly bring our attention to the present and to pull our energy into to a state of equilibrium so that we can separate ourselves from any detrimental or self-limiting thoughts and we can create a space between a stimulus and reaction. This space gives us time to think, breathe, and reflect, so we can consciously decide which energy we need to project to get the most positive outcomes, no matter what the situation is. That space of equilibrium, where we are neither determined or inviting, nor are we light or heavy is a state of mindfulness that I like to call Neutral Energy.

Just like I experienced on the slopes, there are times when being in Neutral Energy may serve you, but there are also times where it might not serve you well. Let's take a look at some examples.

Where projecting Neutral Energy might serve you well

When you project Neutral Energy, you are in an accepting mood. You are the neutral team member who is able to shift

Energy with anyone else in the room. In Neutral Energy, you are instantly adaptable and can work with complete consciousness and mindfulness, so you can be fully present. You are emotionally unmoved by the events that happen in your life, leaving you with energy and vitality to spare.

Three values of projecting Neutral Energy:

1. You bring calmness to the chaos.

    When in Neutral Energy, it is easy for you to tap into your breath and find your centre, even when life gets a little chaotic. During times of crisis or disruption, people will gravitate toward your sense of calm and will come to you for inspiration. Your Neutral Energy is accepting of the Energies around you and that makes people in your team feel safe and comfortable around you. Your accepting nature raises psychological safety in your team, so they feel more comfortable to share ideas, feedback, and concerns with each other and you.

2. You embody acceptance and gratitude.

    In times of change or crisis, people tend to turn to you for advice. Much more than your knowledge, you have the ability to accept any news, feedback, or opinion in a balanced manner. Your deep sense of gratitude helps you glide through your day, no matter what might be happening in your life. In Neutral Energy, you are self-aware and fully present, so you can fully experience every experience and event in your life with total consciousness.

3. You embody authentic leadership.

    Your Neutral Energy helps you accept yourself in any situation. Your self-compassion enables you to speak from the heart, while practicing authentic compassion and care for your people. Your ability to be compassionate, caring, and authentic draws your people in to you. Your authentic aura helps build higher levels of trust in your team and people, and they become inspired to build more authentic relationships with themselves and each other.

Where projecting Neutral Energy might not serve you so well

Projecting a neutral posture all the time can be challenging because you run the risk of being seen as someone who doesn't care about the situation you are in. While in Neutral Energy, your display of emotion and mood could become extremely neutral, making it difficult for people to read where you stand in your opinions and thoughts. This neutrality could lead people to feel disconnected from you while working as a team, and this could lead to distrust.

Being too neutral and unaffected can be a problem if you are stuck in that mood all the time. A lack of perceived care, while not displaying your passion for life and circumstances, could lead people to not feel comfortable around you, and this could lead to a decrease in inclusion at work and in life.

Three challenges while projecting Neutral Energy:

1. You may be viewed as being disinterested.
    In situations that require an Energy that is not Neutral, you may find yourself feeling like a fish out of water. For example, while the team is driving forward with an important initiative, you may find that your Neutral Energy is perceived by the team as being too passive, which could bring the energy of the team down. In such instances, your Neutral Energy may be interpreted as being disinterested or disengaged. Over time, your team members may stop including you in high-energy initiatives, which could result in a breakdown of communication and trust.

2. You may not be able to fully experience life.
    Projecting Neutral Energy may serve you well when calmness inspires confidence. However, your neutral energy may come at a cost if you become stuck in your neutral posture. There are some instances in life where events are best experienced in extreme feelings and energies, such as joy, love, passion, sports, competition, and so on. Becoming stuck in a neutral posture could make you feel

the life's experiences are 'flat', thus reducing the potential of fully experiencing the magical moments of your life.

3. You struggle to multitask.

One fact of modern life is that we live in a culture that requires us to be able to function while performing multiple tasks simultaneously. When in Neutral Energy, your balanced and peaceful nature may decrease your capacity to switch rapidly from one task to another, and to react in a timely manner. Your diminished capacity to quickly switch tasks may cause frustration in your people or team members. Over time, this may result in your team members not including you in dynamic initiatives or high-energy, urgent situations.

Neutral Energy in body-mind-action

A little different from the other Energies, Neutral Energy neither projects Energy, nor does it draw energy in. It is also neither Heavy nor Light. Neutral Energy sits somewhere between the other Energies. It is a space where we can simply be, where we can fully experience the moment we are in, while at the same time, maintaining a level of alertness and readiness that enables us to shift into any of the other energies when required. The previous scenario is a great example of how being too meditative created a deep level of relaxation that lifted me out of my body. It took me so far out of my body that my body lost its capacity to be alert and responsive to the dynamic environment I was in. This was not a state of Neutral Energy because I was not present in my body. True Neutral Energy requires us to be fully present in our mind, but also in the body, so that we can respond with appropriate action where required. Below are some statements that might help identify what being in Neutral Energy might feel like:

1. While being in Neutral Energy, I feel peaceful.
2. In a group setting, I tend to be accepting of everyone and in peaceful thought.
3. In team meetings, I tend to have a calming effect on people.
4. In times of chaos, I am completely unaffected and focus on being centred.

5. In times of conflict, I accept the situation and take no action.
6. My posture becomes relaxed, but centred.
7. I become balanced.
8. My breathing slows down.
9. My face becomes relaxed.
10. My mind is silent.

Scenario Two

As Kilani and I made our way to the ski lift for another round of abuse, I started to practice generating a combination of Determined Energy to get some active Energy flowing through my body, along with Light Energy, so that I could feel lighter on my board and be more adaptable to whatever situation I would come across on the slope. While on the ski lift, I summoned as much Determined Energy as I could to prepare for the dreaded dismount from the ski lift. Moving up the mountain, I purposely sped up my breathing and consciously created tension in my body. I put on my determined face, reduced my peripheral vision, and focused solely on the ski lift dismount area. While I was generating Determined Energy, I visualized myself getting off the lift with balance, grace, and confidence. I visualized the dismount so clearly that I could start feeling my body systems beginning to activate in preparation for the dismount. By the time we reached the ski lift dismount area, I had already played the scenario in my mind at least a dozen times and felt ready for what was to come.

The moment I felt my snowboard touch the snow, I was focused and ready. I pushed off the ski lift chair while perfectly balanced on my board, and I could feel myself glide in perfect harmony with my board, away from the ski lift. When I reached a safe distance, I turned and stopped my board and looked up at Kilani with a massive smile. She reciprocated with two thumbs up and a big smile. Pushing myself to the top of the slope, I felt that being in Light Energy would serve me better because I wanted to have fun and be in a state of adaptability so that I could be prepared for any challenges that might come my way. I took a deep breath and first pulled myself into Neutral Energy so I could release my Determined Energy. Then, I consciously shifted myself into Light Energy by conjuring up feelings of joy, fun, and happiness. I put on the biggest smile possible and with that I imagined myself becoming lighter on my snowboard. I felt as light as a feather as the feelings of joy, fun, and happiness coursed through my body. When ready, I pointed the nose of my board down the slope and gave the board permission to guide me down the slope. With every turn, I could feel a deep connection with my board as my board did what it did best. I felt like it wasn't me controlling the board, but that I was a passenger on top of the board, and we were on one hell of a ride together. It was one of the most exhilarating feelings I had ever felt, and I took in every second of that ride. As the board and I merged energies, we rode down the slope with absolute ease while having an absolute blast.

When I reached the bottom of the slope, I could feel an incredible surge of Energy, and I had the biggest smile on my face. After thirty years of not snowboarding, I had forgotten how much fun it was to surf down a mountain, and I felt tremendously grateful that Kilani asked me to come along on this trip. Needless to say, this was another treasure of an experience, and it was one I will never forget, thanks to Kilani, my board, and my ability to consciously shift energies.

An important takeaway from scenarios one and two is that conscious energy projection and unconscious Energy projection can have very different outcomes. In scenario one, I found myself caught up in my mindful state, loving every minute of being in peace and acceptance. However, because it was not a conscious choice of mine to be there, I failed to activate myself and shift Energy when the situation changed, and activation was required. Critical here is the understanding that what separates conscious Energy from unconscious Energy is the power of choice. When in unconscious Energy, we are not in a position to consciously choose our Energy or to shift wilfully from one Energy to the other. Thus, we may find ourselves in situations where our Energy is not serving us. To be consciously present with our Energy gives us that power of choice so we can respond to whatever situation is before us, projecting the Energy necessary to produce the most impactful outcome. The power of conscious choice lives in a state of Neutral Energy.

As for Neutral Energy, the difference between conscious and unconscious neutrality is the same difference as between being ready and not being ready. Conscious neutrality is a space where we are perfectly balanced and ready. Much like an elite tennis player who is waiting to receive a serve from their opponent. They are not passively waiting for the opponent to serve the ball to their side of the court. Instead, they are at a level of alertness that prepares their body and brain to rapidly—in a fraction of a second—shift into any gear necessary to perform the appropriate response to the serve. That could be receiving the serve with a forehand, with a backhand, or sprinting to a different part of the court before returning the ball. Much like these elite athletes, conscious neutrality should be a state of mindful readiness and alertness, not passiveness.

Practice generating Neutral Energy

Just like the physical movements we practiced to help us generate the other energies, we can do a similar movement to practice generating Neutral Energy. The objective of this exercise is very different from the others. The objective of this exercise is to find your space that sits right in the middle, between the other four energies, where you are relaxed, but also alert and ready.

Just like with the other energy exercises, this exercise can be practiced either sitting down, or standing up. If you are sitting, I want you to sit up straight in your chair. If you are standing, stand with your feet apart, at about hip-width. To start, I want you to focus on your breath, breathing in through your nose and out through your mouth. With every breath in, I want you to fill your lungs and stomach with as much air as you can. When you exhale, relax your jaw, and just let the air flow out of your lungs without any effort.

Now, when you inhale, I want you to place your hands on your stomach, just below your bellybutton. In tai chi, this is referred to as your 'dan tian' and in sports science, this is area is known as your centre of gravity. As you inhale, I want you to push your stomach out against your hands and bring your attention to the point where your hands are making contact with your stomach.

As you exhale, push your stomach back into place using your hands. Note that you are switching your attention from pushing your hands away from your body with your stomach when you inhale, and then pushing your stomach back into place with your hands when you exhale.

Just like with the other energies, incorporating a facial expression is critical to activate the emotional centres. The facial expression of Neutral Energy is complete relaxation around the eyes and face, except for very slight tension in the corners of your mouth. Imagine that you are about to start smiling, but not actually smiling. The tension in the corners of your mouth are going to help your brain maintain an appropriate level of alertness so that you can be ready to consciously choose to shift your energy into any of the other energies depending on the situation.

Just like with the other energy exercises, I want you to repeat this ten times. While you are doing this movement, try to find your state of relaxation while maintaining balance and being mentally and physically alert simultaneously.

After ten repetitions, relax for a moment and observe how the energy in your body and mind has changed from before you started. Take a moment to observe how this exercise feels in your body.

Now that you have practiced all of the energies, I want you to take this to the next level by combining all the energy exercises as a single five-exercise sequence.

If you can't fully remember how to perform each exercise, go back to each chapter that describes the respective exercise for each energy and take some time practicing each individual exercise before attempting the following exercise. It's critical that you master each movement as a sequence before attempting to do this, so that you can get the most out of each movement.

Start in Neutral Energy and take three deep breaths. On your fourth inhalation, bring your hands up to your chest and push yourself into Determined Energy. Try to project as much Determined Energy as you can in that one forward push. As you inhale, draw your hands back to your chest. Exhale and bring yourself back to Neutral Energy with your hands on your stomach. Inhale again and bring your hands up to get ready for Inviting Energy. Exhale and open yourself up into that Inviting Energy. Remember to smile, tilt your head back, and let out that big sigh. On your inhalation, bring your hands back in front of your chest. Exhale back into Neutral Energy, with your hands on your stomach. Inhale again, bringing your hands up and prepare for Light Energy. On your exhalation, press up and project as much joy as you can. Remember to fully embody that joyfulness in face and body. Inhale again, bringing your hands down to your chest. Exhale back into Neutral Energy. Finally, inhale again, bringing your hands up to prepare for Heavy Energy. Exhale and press yourself down into the ground. Inhale again, bringing your hands back up to your chest, and exhale back into neutral, where you started.

As an exercise, perform this sequence five times as a continuous sequence. Once you complete the sequence five times, take a moment to observe yourself. How does your body feel? Some people begin to feel warmer; others feel a tingling sensation through their bodies. Some people feel a lightness. Whatever it is, take a moment to notice how you feel. Then, pay attention to how you feel emotionally. Also, observe your thought patterns. Is your mind quiet but alert? If you can feel this, you have officially found your true Neutral Energy where you are perfectly balanced: relaxed but ready.

From this space, practice voluntarily shifting yourself into any of the energies from Neutral Energy without performing the physical movements described earlier. In time, with practice, it will become easier for you to voluntarily shift your Energy.

Wellness concerns of Neutral Energy

As I mentioned earlier, Neutral Energy is characterized by being balanced, relaxed, but ready. Finding your Neutral Energy may feel extremely comforting and healing for you as it is a place where you are present in the now, where you are fully alert, and accepting of your situation, but you are also completely unaffected by it. This sensation can become so comforting that it may become a little addictive for some people and where it becomes a desired state. The problem with this is that fully experiencing the wonders of life doesn't happen in Neutral Energy but in the other energies. Neutral Energy is meant to be a temporary holding cell. A small space that allows us to consciously shift our energy from one to the other. Holding on to any one energy, including Neutral Energy, for too long can have negative effects on your well-being. The greatest wellness gift that you can give yourself is to learn to be conscious about how much time you are spending in each of the Energies and to practice moving yourself back into Neutral Energy after each bout of any of the other Energies.

Below are some challenges that you could encounter when you spend too much time trying to be in Neutral Energy:

1. Life can feel flat when spending too much time in Neutral Energy.
2. Being neutral reduces the capacity for accessing your intuition and wisdom.
3. Being neutral for too long may result in become detached from people.
4. Being neutral for too long may result in stress from social isolation.
5. Being neutral may reduce your capacity for innovation and creativity.
6. Being neutral may reduce your capacity to feel passionate about people.
7. Being neutral for too long can cause lethargy.
8. Being in Neutral Energy may reduce your capacity to be playful.

Now, you've been introduced to all five of the Energies and have had some time to practice each of them in body, mind, and action. You will likely have identified that there were one or two that were very comfortable for you and that the others were harder for you to connect with. If that's the case, that's totally normal. What this means is that you are already more practiced in the one or two energies that you are most comfortable with, and are less practiced in the others.

Just like with anything else in life, we get better with practice. Give yourself some time to practice the Energies you are less comfortable with, until shifting from one Energy to another begins to feel more natural. In the next chapter, we are going to do an assessment to help you assess which of the Energies is the one you project the most in various situations in your life.

Chapter 13

Assess Yourself

About ten years ago, I was approached by another global fitness chain to help them in their expansion into Asia. As the largest gym franchise in the world, their revenue does not come from selling memberships and conducting revenue generating services alone, but also from the sale of franchises. A very ambitious move from this global chain was to open franchises in six countries simultaneously. As one of the first hires for this project, I found myself part of a three-person leadership team that was tasked with building the entire infrastructure across these six countries. One of our strategies was to recruit and train a leadership team in each of the countries where we were planning to operate.

As a so-called expert in gym operations, one of my many jobs during the initial setup period, long before the first gym was opened, was to construct a leadership development model that would help support the members of each country's leadership team. As each country's leadership team became operational and they began selling franchises to franchisees, I started receiving feedback from the leadership teams that they needed support in learning how to coach their franchisees to be more effective gym operators, so that they would be set up for success once their gyms were open. Despite the fact that this franchise company had incredibly elaborate brand compliance and operations procedures that had a credible track record around the globe, and despite the fact that each franchise gym was a large financial commitment for each franchisee, many franchisees struggled with working within the exact procedural boundaries prescribed by the company. All too often, franchisees would have their own ideas about how they wanted to operate their businesses and would often push back hard on the regulations set by the company, even when they had no experience operating a fitness business.

In hindsight, this is totally understandable. On one hand, investing in, and running a franchise requires a tremendous entrepreneurial mindset. On the other hand, operating a franchise also requires a large degree of compliance to operational and branding procedures that are dictated by the franchise. The type of franchisees who possessed the capital to open a fitness franchise were, in most cases, already highly successful entrepreneurs who had already built highly profitable businesses while doing things their own way. On one hand, their experience in taking calculated risks and building businesses was a tremendous advantage. However, their successful track records and experience in other industries raised the opportunity for the cultivation of a strong bias towards how they believed a fitness franchise needed to be built, despite the fact that they had never built a successful fitness franchise before.

I remember, one day, being in a conversation with my Singapore leadership team about the coachability of their franchisees in Singapore. The person in charge of the leadership team himself was an extremely successful fitness franchisee who owned a chain of fitness franchises in Australia. He had built his own fitness empire through hard work and by blindly following the franchise procedures put in place by the franchise company. He was highly enthusiastic about the franchise business and badly wanted every franchisee in Singapore to enjoy the same success as he did. Unfortunately, his success as a fitness franchisee in Australia had not prepared him to be a successful leader of franchisees in Singapore; but from his own success, he had developed his own bias about how franchisees should be led. During our coffee, he was telling me about how worried he was about some of his franchisees because they weren't listening to him and not doing what he was telling them to do. He felt that franchisees in Singapore were not coachable. When I asked him what it means to be coachable, he told me that for a franchisee to be coachable, they must be compliant and willing to do what he tells them to do. I then went on to ask him what he thought might be causing the resistance in his franchisees against following his directions.

He told me that he believed that the type of franchisee in Singapore was different from that in Australia in that franchisees there were much more coachable. I then asked him how many franchisees he was leading in Australia. He told me that he wasn't leading any franchisees in Australia, but he knew many of them, and all of them were extremely coachable.

I then went to visit all of the franchisees in Singapore to ask them about how they felt about being coachable. After visiting each franchisee, it became clear to me that the problem was not with the franchisees, but with the leader. Each franchisee was extremely forthcoming with me and they all described the leader as an extremely determined leader. In his Determined Energy, the leader had a tendency to aggressively enforce his ideas and assumptions on his franchisees. He was so extremely passionate about his own thoughts and ideas that he would not entertain any feedback or suggestions from his franchisees. This breakdown in communication drove a wedge in the trust of the franchisees, and with that, many decided to just ignore the leader and run their businesses the best way they knew how. As time went on and the franchisees complied less and less with the leader's aggressive style of leading, the leader reciprocated by becoming more and more determined in his energy, to a point where he was beginning to yell at the franchisees to make them comply, which only made things worse.

A few days later, I was speaking with my colleague, the Chief Operating Officer of this global fitness chain. He used to be a corporate trainer before taking on the role of COO. I explained to him what was happening in Singapore and told him I was not sure how to have a conversation with the leader about how he is behaving with his franchisees. I felt that he was so stuck in his belief system, he may be resistant to feedback. My COO friend suggested that if I didn't think having a direct feedback conversation with the leader would be fruitful, maybe I should look into using some form of psychometric assessment that could spark a conversation around the effectiveness of his leadership and communication style.

The COO shared with me that during his years as a corporate trainer, he worked with an assessment that he had developed. He had seen great results when leaders became aware that their leadership style was only one option of many different styles. With that awareness, they often became more open to exploring if other leadership styles could produce greater results.

He then shared the assessment with me and I went with that tool to my franchise leader in Singapore, who was very willing to give it a go. After completing the assessment, I discovered that he was extremely directive and forceful in his way of leading, which could be interpreted as being aggressive. Once he became aware that a different approach may produce better results with his franchisees, the franchise leader opened himself to the idea and agreed that he would be willing to undergo coaching himself, so that he could practice learning to apply himself differently for the benefit of his franchisees.

One of the first coaching conversations I had with the Singapore franchise leader was to define what being coachable really means. As I mentioned earlier, his personal understanding was that being coachable meant to be compliant and willing to do as you are told. I then presented him with the definition that has been stipulated by the International Coaching Federation, an organization that sets the global standard in coaching. The ICF defines coaching as partnering with clients in a thought-provoking and creative process that inspires them to maximize their personal and professional potential. As I presented that definition to him, I asked him which words from this definition jumped out at him. He looked up at me and said, 'Partnering and Inspires.' I let him sit with that for a bit and he said, 'I can do that. I can partner with my franchisees and inspire them at the same time.' I then asked him how life could be different for him if he was successful at creating a stronger partnership with his franchisees. He immediately realized that life would be a lot more peaceful, and that franchisees would probably be a lot happier and maybe even more profitable too.

A few weeks later, I received a call from the franchise leader, and he told me that he had seen incredible results from his assessment, both in himself and how it made an incredible difference in his relationship with his franchisees. He was so impressed that he has been sharing it with the franchisees as well, who in turn found it very useful in understanding how they were leading their respective staff. The positive effects of a simple assessment didn't stop there. The franchise managers, trainers, and sales staff all started using the assessment to help them in their respective jobs. Managers used it to help them understand how to be a better communicator with their members. The sales staff used the assessment to better understand the communication styles of their prospective members. And finally, the trainers started using it to better understand how they could be more effective personal trainers.

This experience was my first experience where I got to see the powerful potential of something that is so simple as a questionnaire. In that experience, I had the privilege of witnessing the effects of the intervention trickle from the top an organization all the way down to the bottom. Little did I know back then that this experience would inspire an idea within me which, after a decade, has evolved into a full-fledged leadership coaching model.

In similar fashion, I would like to share this Five Energies Questionnaire with you to help you identify what your default energy might be throughout your day. And just like in the scenario above, I'm hoping you will be able to use this to help you understand your own operating mode better, while also developing a deeper understanding of your staff, your own managers, prospective clients, and yes, even your loved ones at home. Once you develop a decent understanding of how you and other people are projecting energy, you can begin to practice using this skill as a way to connect with people at a much deeper level.

So, how does this questionnaire work? Below, you will find a series of ten groups of statements. Each statement group consists of five statements. Each statement within each group will represent one of the five energies: determined, light, inviting, heavy, and neutral. What I would like you to do is read each statement within each statement group carefully. Select the statement in each group that you feel most relates to you. I recommend highlighting each statement that best fits you. After each statement, you will see in brackets the respective energy they connect to.

Once you complete highlighting each statement that represents you, I will share how to use the scores to identify which is your default energy.

Here's what not to do. It can be extremely tempting to select the statement that you aspire to be or that you think others will want to see in you. Remember, this is your assessment and yours alone. Nobody's looking right now. Be honest and truthful with yourself. This will help you create a more accurate picture of your default energy. Remember, there is no right or wrong energy. As you read in the previous chapters, each energy serves us really well in some cases, but not so well in others. This assessment will simply help you identify the energy that you are more likely to project in any situation.

Ready? Here we go!

1.   Choose the one statement that is most like you.

I am Talkative.	(Light)
I am Daring.	(Determined)
I am Loyal.	(Inviting)
I am Reserved.	(Heavy)
I am Peaceful.	(Neutral)

2.   How do other people see you?

People come to me for solutions.	(Heavy)
People see me as having a calming influence.	(Neutral)
People see me as being helpful.	(Inviting)
People usually like my company.	(Light)
People tend to look up to me.	(Determined)

3.   What role do you play in a team setting?

I ensure a strong team synergy.	(Light)
I like to focus on the task at hand.	(Heavy)
I just wait and open myself to ideas from others.	(Inviting)
I focus inward on my well-being and let others figure things out.	(Neutral)
I like to drive initiatives and lead the way.	(Determined)

4. Choose the one statement that you feel is most like you.

    I am disciplined.   (Heavy)
    I am entertaining.   (Light)
    I am dominant.   (Determined)
    I am neutral.   (Neutral)
    I am patient.   (Inviting)

5. Choose the one statement that you feel is most like you.

    I am balanced.   (Neutral)
    I am cooperative.   (Inviting)
    I am charming.   (Light)
    I am decisive.   (Determined)
    I am reserved.   (Heavy)

6. Choose the one statement that you feel is most like you.

    I am fearless.   (Determined)
    I am sociable.   (Light)
    I am generous.   (Inviting)
    I am analytical.   (Heavy)
    I am impartial.   (Neutral)

7. You are in a team working on a project. Which statement is
    most like you?

    I tend to be systematic in my approach to tasks.   (Heavy)
    I prefer to remain silent and just follow along.   (Neutral)
    I like to be bold in my actions and decisions.   (Determined)
    I like to nurture my team members and   (Inviting)
    enjoy seeing their growth.
    I like to influence people's mood   (Light)
    so that everyone gets along.

8.   Choose the one statement that you feel is most like you.

  I am very active, both at work and play.   (Determined)
  I am always cheerful.   (Light)
  I always take notice of what other people say.   (Inviting)
  I am unbiased when people   (Neutral)
  share their opinions.
  I like to behave correctly and follow protocol.   (Heavy)

9.   There's a conflict in your team. How do you react?

  Let's not upset anyone.   (Light)
  Let's hear more details.   (Heavy)
  I focus on my own well-being and wait for   (Neutral)
  the issue to pass.
  Let's just get straight to the point.   (Determined)
  Let's all talk it out.   (Inviting)

10. Choose one statement that you feel is most like you.

  I'm a good listener.   (Inviting)
  I enjoy socializing with people.   (Light)
  I enjoy competition.   (Determined)
  I like to be strategic.   (Heavy)
  I live my life in a balanced manner.   (Neutral)

Now that you are done, you should have highlighted only one statement within each of the ten groups of statements. Take a moment to go back to the statements and add how many determined statements you chose and write the number down. Do the same for the light statements, inviting statements, heavy statements, and finally neutral statements.

To interpret the results, look at the energy type that got the highest number. That will be your most common energy projection. The second highest number will be your second most common energy projection and so on. For example, if you scored four determined, one light, one inviting, three heavy, and one neutral, that means that your default energy projection is determined, followed by heavy. In that case, you are likely to find yourself shifting from Determined Energy to Heavy Energy more than the other energies. On the flipside, you likely spend the least amount of time in light, inviting, and neutral energies.

With this awareness, go back to the two chapters that explain your top two energies. Take a look at how these energies can serve you well, but also how these energies may not serve you sometimes.

Conversely, also take a look at the chapters that explain your bottom two energies. How might the absence of these two energies be getting in the way of you being at your best? Are there situations that show up in your day where you would benefit from projecting a different energy than your two most common energies? If the answer is yes, then the next chapter is going to be very helpful for you.

In the next chapter, we are going to explore how to consciously shift your energy, so that you can become the best version of yourself in any situation in your life.

Chapter 14

The Art of Shifting Energy

.

Famous 20th century humourist, P.G. Wodehouse once said, 'To find a person's true character, play golf with them.' What he meant was that who we are shows up in very obvious ways through how we act in any aspect of life. Whether it's when we're playing a game like golf, acting as parents or spouses, or acting at the workplace, we behave in certain ways that have become so natural to us that we don't notice them ourselves, but to the rest of the world, those ways of acting stand out like a sore thumb.

As I mentioned in Chapter 4, we all have automatic behaviours, ways of operating, that sometimes serve us well, and sometimes do not. Yet, because these behaviours are so automatic that making them visible to us is not always that easy; in some cases, becoming aware of them can be painful or embarrassing. In the previous chapters, you had an opportunity to identify your default way of projecting energy. The outcome of this self-assessment may have come as a big surprise to you, or it may just have revealed to you what you already know about yourself. Either way, having a greater awareness of your default energy projection is the first step towards helping you shift energy when required.

In this chapter, I'd like to invite you to do something a little more radical. Rather than just being more aware and staying in the comfort of your own energy projection, I would like to invite you to do some fun experiments on yourself to see whether projecting different energies could produce different results for you. Of course, this need not be applied only at work, but can be applied in any aspect of your life. You can apply this in your relationships with your loved ones. You can apply it while learning something new. You can even apply it while exercising. No matter what you do in your life, you are projecting at least one of the five energies, at any given moment.

Once you become more comfortable practicing the different energies in different scenarios, I'm going to share with you how you can use that skill to become a more positive influence in the lives of others, such as the people you work with and the people you live with. This skill will not only help you get along better with people, but you will become more effective in your ability to communicate, negotiate, and collaborate with anyone.

Are you ready? Let's get started!

Step 1: Observe yourself in your current energy.

In Chapters 8 to 12, you had the opportunity to learn more about each type of energy projection. In each of those chapters, I highlighted how energy projection can show up in body, mind, and action. For example, when in Determined Energy, energy projection that is characterized as forward moving, our bodies, our thoughts and feelings, and our actions differ from when we are in the other energies. To effectively observe yourself in body-mind-action, imagine watching yourself from outside of your body. Position yourself in a place where you have good visibility of how you are showing up. Ask yourself some critical questions from each of the body-mind-action categories.

What I would like to stress here is that you do not need to diagnose yourself. The type of energy you might be projecting unconsciously is going to be different from the type of energy you will be projecting consciously. So, diagnosing your unconscious energy will not produce any effective results. Instead, simply observe how you are showing up in that given moment, and that's all you need to do in the first step.

Three Body Awareness Questions:

1. What is my body doing right now?

As you observe yourself from a distance, take a look at how your body is behaving. Is it making large forceful movements? Is it bouncing in excitement? Or is it sitting completely still? From the outside in, do a scan of your body's internal systems. How is your heart rate? Is it rapid or slow? How about your breathing? Are you breathing in a shallow pattern from your chest, or are you breathing deeply that includes your stomach? How much tension do you feel in your body? Is your body tense, or is your body relaxed?

How about any tingling sensations? Is there perhaps any pain in your body? If there is, where is this pain? Temperature is another one to look out for. Are you starting to feel warm or are you feeling cold?

There are countless observations we can make about what our bodies might be doing and how our bodies might be behaving in any given situation. Paying attention without judgment helps bring our attention to ourselves, so that we can begin to consciously choose how we want our bodies to behave.

2. What's the posture of my body?
    Aikido Grandmaster Morihei Ueshiba once said, 'A good stance and posture reflect a proper state of mind.' When observing your stance and posture, take note of your legs. If you are standing, how are you positioning your legs and feet? Are you standing in a way where you feel you are ready for a fight, or are you standing loosely and comfortably? If you are sitting, observe your legs too. Are your legs comfortably leaving your chair, or are they stiff and tight? Are your legs crossed, spread open, or are they positioned close together under your hips?

    From your legs, move your attention to your spine and to your shoulders. Is your spine straight or is it rounded? How about your shoulders? Are your shoulders relaxed and hanging loosely below your ears or are they tight and propped up toward your ears? Are your shoulders rounded and slouching forward?

3. What's my facial expression?
    Ground-breaking research from Dr Paul Ekman has taught us that the use facial expressions to convey emotions and feelings are universal across all cultures. What this can teach us is that no matter

how different some people in this world think that people from other races, cultures, and genders are, we all express how we feel in the same ways.

However, in my years of coaching managers, I have come across many professionals who struggle to identify with how they are feeling. Many professionals have taught themselves over decades of corporate life that emotions only get in the way of productivity and profitability. For them, learning to ignore their own feelings served them to a point, until they became bosses and leaders themselves.

Most emerging leaders now are learning the importance of emotional intelligence in leadership and for some, this means re-teaching themselves how to become more comfortable working with emotions, rather than suppressing them.

One of the problems of suppressing emotions is that over time, it becomes more difficult for such a person to read the emotional expressions of others. As the reader, you may have no problem with reading facial expressions in others, but I bet you can pinpoint a number of people you work with who do struggle to recognize how a person might be feeling based on their expressions.

A simple way of learning to recognize facial expressions is by starting with recognizing your own expressions by systematically scanning your face.

Start by scanning your eyebrows. Are your eyebrows raised, neutral, or lowered? Another observation that you can make with your eyebrows is whether your eyebrows are arched or drawn in toward each other.

From your eyebrows, move your attention to your eyes. Are your eyes open, neutral, or squinting? How about your focus? Is your focus very narrow, or is it very broad, where you can take in a lot of peripheral vision?

From your eyes, scan downward to your mouth and jaw. Is your mouth open or closed? Are you smiling? Are your lips pursed or is your mouth closed, with one side of your mouth raised above the other? How about your jaw? Do you feel tension in your jaw, or are you perhaps clenching your teeth? Or are your jaw feeling relaxed and comfortable?

Remember that no matter what you observe in yourself, you do not need to diagnose yourself at this point. Whatever your body is telling you, there is no right or wrong way of expressing itself. Just observe how your body is behaving in the situation that you are in and take note of that awareness.

Three mind awareness questions:

1. What is my mood right now?
    Have you ever woken up in the morning and noticed that you were in a really good mood? You may also have witnessed yourself waking up in a really foul mood. How about being invited to a dinner party and just not feeling 'in the mood' for it? There are also probably times when you were in a super productive mood and could get tons of work done. There will be instances where you were in a really adventurous mood. Conversely, you may also have experienced yourself attending a lengthy presentation that just did not interest you, where you were feeling super bored. All of these examples are examples of moods that likely happen to every single one of us at some point of time. The reason why this is relevant is because moods, like emotions, strongly influence how we show up in the world and therefore play a significant role in the energy we are projecting. One question I often receive from my coaching clients is, 'What's the difference between mood and emotion?' Well, many people tend to use the terms mood and emotion interchangeably, but understanding how they are related and how they differ will help you identify your own moods, and thus your own energy.

    In their ground-breaking book, *The Nature of Emotions*, authors Ekman and Davidson highlighted that even though moods, emotions, and temperament are bound together, they do differ in a number of ways. Most notably, emotion is a short-lived feeling, it can stay, maybe, for a few minutes, whereas mood is a feeling that can last for hours, days, or even weeks.

In his book, *Positive Intelligence*, author Shirzad Chamine uses the example of placing your hand on a hot stove top. From the moment when your hand touches the hot stove to the moment you pull your hand away from the stove in pain could be seen as the length of an emotion that is triggered in response to a clear stimulus, in this case a stove top. Moods, on the other hand, tend to last longer and are not present so evidently. However, what makes a mood significant is that our moods have a tendency to set the tone for how we interpret and respond to our environments.

For example, If I am assigned to attend a workshop today that I didn't want to attend and I walk into the workshop in a mood of resentment, judgement, or boredom, I will likely pay less attention during the lessons and therefore get less out of the workshop, which in turn will only reinforce to me why I was right in not wanting to attend the workshop in the first place. On the other hand, if I attend a workshop in a mood of curiosity, excitement, wonder, and adventure, I'll likely get more out of it.

What this means is that our moods don't only set the tone for how we are going to experience our situations, they also dictate how we are going to think and act in our situations. Each mood that you have is going to drive you to project a certain energy. For example, if you are bored, will your energy be light or heavy? If you are in a productive mood, which energy are you more likely to project? You will likely be projecting more Determined Energy. How about being in a really loving or compassionate mood? Yes, you will likely be projecting more inviting or Light Energy.

So, as part of your self-awareness practice, try waking up in the morning and see if you can recognize the mood you wake up in, each day. Also, when you show up at work, or in a meeting, give yourself a moment to scan your mood so you can make sure you are fully conscious of the mood in which you are going into a certain situation.

2. What are my thoughts saying?
As I highlighted before, we have many thousands of thoughts each day. Some of these thoughts might serve us extremely well. On the

other hand, they may not serve us so well in some circumstances. What is interesting to note here is that your thoughts are directly related to the mood you're in and your mood, in return, influences your thoughts. In their book, *Individual Therapy Manual for Cognitive-Behavioral Treatment of Depression,* authors Drs Ricardo Munoz and Jeanne Miranda explain that thoughts are nothing more than ideas or stories that we tell ourselves. Some of these stories are very automatic in nature, meaning that they run around in our heads constantly. If a person's automatic thought process is depressing in nature, it will stimulate a depressed mood, whereas thoughts that are uplifting and full of possibility can decrease a person's depressed mood.

Earlier, I used an example of going into a workshop that I didn't want to attend and thus walked into the workshop in a mood of resentment, judgement, or boredom. In that mood, I may find myself thinking thoughts like, 'I don't want to be here,' or 'This is so boring,' or 'I'm getting nothing out of this.' By filling my mind with these thoughts, I stop paying attention to the material that is being taught. At the end of the workshop, I will then walk out of it, having learned nothing because I was too busy thinking about all the reasons why I wasn't learning anything. Walking away from that workshop, I may then start thinking about how right I was to not want to go to that workshop because it didn't teach me anything new, just as I had predicted. At that moment, I risk developing a phenomenon called 'confirmation bias' or simply put, proving myself right.

The next time I am asked to attend a similar workshop, my bias is going to tell me that, again, I am not going to learn anything and that this workshop is going to be really boring again. So, what do you think my mood will be walking into the new workshop? I likely won't be in a mood that is very open to learning.

3. What am I feeling?

    If I received a dollar for every boss and leader who told me that feelings do not belong in business, I'd be an extremely wealthy man. Time and time again, I hear from these executives that in the course of their careers, they were trained to put their feelings aside for the sake of the company. This may seem like a pragmatic approach to keeping a clear head in times when tough decisions need to be made; however, where this strategy falls short is that as a human being, you are designed to feel. When thinking that we can ignore our feelings, we are not actually putting our feelings aside; instead, we are simply operating in a mood of denial. Being in a mood of denial doesn't mean that we don't show our emotions or feelings; on the contrary, the more we try to deny or suppress our feelings, the more they show up to the world, without us being aware of the damage unchecked emotions might have on the organization. As a boss or leader, you tell me what is more detrimental for a business: a boss who lacks awareness of their feelings, or a boss who is acutely aware, emotionally articulate and capable of leveraging off them?

Earlier in this book, I spoke about how our energies play a certain tune and the vibrations resulting from that tune set the tone for the type of affect we have on our people and the type of weather we create within the organization. Your emotions and feelings not only play a significant role in the type of tune you are vibrating to in your environment, but they also function as a volume button for your tune. The more this is going on inside you emotionally, the stronger the vibrations you are sending out into the world around you and these are received by the people in your surroundings at higher intensities.

One question I hear a lot from my clients is, 'How do I work with my feelings?' That's a really good question, but not the most important question to start with. The most important question to ask yourself is, 'What can I do to be more aware of my feelings?' The answer to that question is simple. Pay attention!

Daniel Goleman, the man who helped us appreciate emotional intelligence once said, 'Out-of-control emotions make a smart man stupid.' This also holds true for unchecked emotions and feelings. A technique commonly used in emotional awareness training by psychologists is called 'affect labelling'. What this means is that when you feel something, you simply give it a name. If you feel pain, say to yourself, 'I feel pain.' If you feel anger, say to yourself: 'I feel angry,' and so on. Research in development psychology has taught us that infants and young children are very good at recognizing that they feel something. They will express what they feel, and once expressed, they will move on and go back to playing and having fun. What we can learn from this observation is that suffering as a result of what we feel is a learned behaviour. The more we deny or suppress how we feel, the more we end up suffering. On the other hand, when we pay attention to what we are feeling and give it a name, our suffering becomes less.

What I learned from years of working with leaders is that when most bosses or leaders try to keep feelings and emotions out of the conversation, what they are trying to do is minimize the suffering that could potentially reduce performance and productivity of the team. What they are often not aware of is that by trying to eliminate the conversation around emotions and feelings altogether, they actually set the stage for even greater suffering within themselves and in their people. Not the best strategy.

By paying attention to the emotions and feelings of ourselves and our people, and by giving ourselves and our people permission to recognize them and name them, we significantly reduce the potential for suffering and provide an avenue for ourselves and our people to move on sooner.

Here's a simple exercise for you to practice labelling your feelings and emotions. Right now, while you are reading this book, take a moment to pay attention to how you feel at this moment. You might be feeling curious. You might be feeling a little judgmental. You may be feeling irritable. On the other hand, you may be feeling peaceful or accepting. No matter what the feeling or emotion is right now, identify with that feeling or emotion by giving it a name and then simply give yourself permission to move on after acknowledging its presence. You do not need to investigate who or what is causing the feeling or create a big story around the causes of the feelings. Simply remove yourself from all of that and just label the feeling. Say something like, 'Right now, I feel curious,' or 'Right now, I feel happy,' or 'Right now, my butt's feeling numb after sitting and reading this book for so long.' Whatever you are feeling right at this moment in time, label it and move on.

Three Action Awareness Questions:

1. What am I doing right now?

    As I've highlighted a number of times already, there is a major difference between conscious and unconscious behaviour. Our ability to be consciously connected to our actions and inactions provides us with a world of knowledge about who we are in different situations. Interesting research by Dr Tasha Eurich, who is an organizational psychologist and the author of the bestselling book *Insight: The Surprising Truth About How Others See Us, How We See Ourselves, and Why the Answers Matter More Than We Think*, says that even though self-awareness is a critical skill in leadership, only about 10 to 15 per cent of the leaders she researched demonstrated actual self-awareness. What's surprising about this is that when presented with the question, whether they think they possess self-awareness, the majority of the bosses and leaders will tell you that they think they have great self-awareness. What this means is that there seems to be a disconnect between the amount of self-awareness we think we have and the amount of self-awareness we actually have. The painful truth of this research is that both you and I probably have much less self-awareness than we think we have.

    One technique that can help us be more self-aware of our actions and inactions is through self-observation. Research in the field of psychology has proven that when patients recall a painful memory from the perspective of an observer who is observing their experience, the emotional pain is significantly reduced. In the same manner, when we practice observing ourselves as an outside observer, much like when we observe people on a TV show, we can reduce the emotional attachment we might be having with what we are doing.

    Let's go back to that example earlier of me being resentful about having to attend that workshop I don't want to attend. I can observe myself as if I am watching myself on TV. I can observe my body-language when walking into the workshop or while attending it. I can observe my facial expressions when the instructor is speaking. I can also observe the tone that I use when

I am speaking. Am I using a resentful tone in my choice of words or am I using a tone of curiosity? What do I look like when I am resentful as opposed to when I am curious?

Now, let's put that into the context of the five energies. What are some behavioural habits that become visible for you when you observe yourself projecting each of the five energies? How do you behave when you are in Determined Energy, for example? What is your way of communicating? What does your voice sound like when you are determined?

In time, with practice, you will learn how to recognize behavioural patterns and actions that keep coming back in each of the five energies, which will make it easier for you to consciously shift from one energy to the other.

2. What do I hope to accomplish by my actions?

While you are observing yourself and you are witnessing your actions and inactions in any situations, a good follow-up question to ask is, 'What do I hope to accomplish by this action?' This question will help put you in a state of forward thinking. Is this way of being and this energy I am projecting getting me the results that I want in this situation?

Going back to the example from earlier, when I was in that workshop, I could have asked myself that same question after observing myself in real time without being emotionally invested in how I was acting. While observing myself feeling resentment, as I had to be in a workshop that was not interesting me, I could have asked myself, 'What do I hope to accomplish while being stuck in my own resentment or suffering?' At that moment in time, I wouldn't really need to know the answer to that question. That question would likely have raised my awareness in real time to understand that there might be a better alternative out there, rather than wasting the day trying to prove to myself that I was right in thinking that I wouldn't learn anything new.

3. What other actions might serve me better?

This brings us to our third question and follows up immediately from the awareness created by the previous two questions. If I were in that workshop and I had the awareness to ask myself what actions, other than acting in a mood of resentment, could serve me better, I may have been able to open myself up to the prospect that I could have learned something new, despite not wanting to attend the workshop. This final question could have been the invitation to move myself into a different energy that would serve me better than the one I was unconsciously in.

With this new observational power, you can begin to map out for yourself what some of your default ways of thinking, feeling, and acting are in the five energies, which in turn provides you with the choice to consciously continue how you are operating, or to make a change for yourself.

Step 2: Shift yourself into Neutral Energy

Once you are more aware of what you were previously not aware of—your way of being in a certain scenario—you can then make a conscious choice to shift yourself into a different energy state that might serve you better. Before you can do that, you must first shift yourself into Neutral Energy. Chris Balsley, a master of somatic integration in leadership and author of *Stop Controlling, Start Leading,* uses the analogy of shifting gears while driving a car. In one of his many engaging lectures through the Newfield Network, Chris described shifting dispositions, or energy, like shifting gears in a manual car. And I can't think of a more fitting analogy than his. If you've ever had the privilege of driving a manual car, you'll know what it's like to have to put your gear shift into neutral before shifting into any other gear. So, when you are standing at a red traffic light, your car will be in first gear. Once the light turns green, you will push your foot down onto the gas pedal, and your car will begin to drive.

The moment you overcome inertia and your car is moving, you will need to put your car into second gear to be able to keep accelerating. The way you do this is by pushing your foot down on the clutch and manually pulling the gearshift into neutral, a space between the other gears. From there, with your foot still on the clutch, you can then push the gearshift into second gear. You can then lift your foot off the clutch and step on the gas so the car can continue accelerating. You will then repeat this action each time you shift to a different gear.

What is relevant with this is to note that neutral is a space where nothing really happens. The car simply glides along while it is in neutral. You do not use it to move forward or backward, you simply use it as a step between gears.

With this analogy in mind, Neutral Energy works in the same way. Neutral Energy is exactly the name says: it is neutral. While you are in Neutral Energy, you are not moving forward, backward, up, or down. While in Neutral Energy, you are ready to move into a different gear. In Chapter 11, I explained the techniques of moving yourself into Neutral Energy and offered some practical exercises to help you bring your Energy into a neutral state. Practicing these exercises will help you become more comfortable shifting yourself into Neutral Energy, and with practice, you will find that it becomes even easier.

What's most important to remember in this situation is that Neutral Energy is the energy state we want to attain before moving ourselves into any other energy state.

In Chapter 11, I used the example of a tennis player being ready to receive the serve from their opponent and that Neutral Energy is the energy of readiness, not passiveness. Let us use that same tennis player as an example. If you ever watch elite tennis players in a rally against each other, you'll probably notice how each player runs back to the middle of the baseline, immediately after hitting the ball back to the other side. No matter what direction that tennis player needs to run to meet the ball, whether they run forward, backward, left, or right, they immediately run back to the centre of the baseline. This is because it is the sweet spot that gives the player equal distance between the left side and the right side of the court, while also putting enough distance between them, the net and the other player, so that they get the most amount of time to respond to whatever ball is hit toward them.

In a very similar fashion, we use Neutral Energy as the sweet spot that gives us the most amount of space to respond to our environment and make conscious choices about how we want to act in that situation. So instead of seeing Neutral Energy as an energy state that you aspire to hold on to, see it more as an Energy state that allows you to transition from one of the other four Energy states to another. So, what this means is that you are only in Neutral Energy when you are deciding which of the other four Energy states to shift into, or when you are moving back to your sweet spot after acting in one of the other four Energy states.

Step 3: Shift yourself into the desired Energy state

In a recent conversation with my client, Dave, he mentioned to me that he was exploring a possible jump to another industry. After working for twenty-three years in the banking industry, my client was considering a job change to work as the chief operating officer for a global fitness chain. In his own industry, Dave was considered somewhat of a rock star, who was well sought after as a mover and a driver of organizational development and growth initiatives.

During our meeting, Dave explained to me that he was an ultra-endurance athlete and was really passionate about fitness. The idea of driving profit in an industry he was passionate about was very appealing to him. I asked him what he felt was his greatest strength that he could take to the fitness company. He told me about how driven he was as a leader and had great success leading with an iron will. 'When targets need to be met, I push my people hard to exceed them,' he said. 'I know this industry in and out and I know how to get results. I can be very caring as a leader, but one thing I cannot tolerate is complacency and incompetence.' Upon hearing that, I asked him what type of energy he thought he projected at work.

After thinking about that for a minute, he identified that he spent most of his time driving people and processes with Determined Energy. 'I'm not only like that at work,' he said, 'I'm also like that in my own training when I'm preparing for a race.'

After listening to this, I asked him, 'Would you approach your new role with the same Determined Energy?' He thought about that and said that he absolutely would. The whole reason why this global fitness chain was interested in him was because he could produce results.

I then asked him whether stepping into a new industry with mostly Determined Energy would serve him best. 'Wouldn't moving into a new industry require some sort of a learning curve?' I asked him. He agreed. I then asked him, which energy state might allow him to be more open to learning. He looked at me for a moment and then said, 'I think it will be Inviting Energy.' I then asked him, how practiced he felt he was in Inviting Energy. 'Not that practiced,' he confessed.

He then realized that if he was going to jump industry, he would need to become more practiced at projecting the other energies, and not just trust bulldozing his way through any challenge using Determined Energy. He then ended the session agreeing to practice shifting himself into other energies so that he could become more agile in projecting his energy when he would make the jump.

Much like any other skill in life, shifting energy is a skill that requires practice. As a practice, it doesn't matter which energy you choose, you need to practice all of them. A great exercise is to monitor yourself consciously throughout your day and try to identify when you are in your default posture. Throughout your day, try practicing shifting yourself into Neutral Energy first, and then, voluntarily moving yourself into a different energy using the exercises you have practiced in Chapters 7 to 11. In time, and with practice, you will start to become more aware of the energy state you are in, how to move yourself into Neutral Energy, and then how to shift yourself into one of the other energies.

Shifting other people into a different energy state

So far, the focus of this chapter has been on shifting your own energy. Now that you are more aware and more practiced in shifting your own energy, let's shift focus from working on yourself to using your newfound skills to help others shift their energies when required.

In my coaching practice working with managers and leaders, one question that I am often asked is, 'How do I use the five energies to help other people shift to a more desired posture?' Using the five energies successfully in communication and negotiation can certainly lead to helping other people see different perspectives and even open themselves up to other possibilities. Using the five energies to be a positive influence in the lives of others and to help them see other possibilities and perspectives can be practiced by using a simple acronym called N.I.C.E.R.: neutral first, inspect, connect, engage, and re-posture.

1. Neutral first

   Just like when you practice shifting energy yourself, it's critical to apply this skill while communicating with other people. Initially, try practicing shifting yourself into Neutral Energy prior to your meeting. Before you speak with the person, take a few deep breaths and practice finding your own neutral posture so you can go into the meeting or conversation in a state of acceptance, balance, and peace while being unmoved by the energy that is projected by others in the meeting.

2. Inspect

   In this step, take a moment to observe your meeting partner(s) and yourself. What is your own energy in the presence of this person's energy? Do you feel an involuntary shift in your own energy? If yes, shift yourself back into Neutral Energy. Then, inspect your meeting partner in the manner in which you practiced observing yourself. Observe your meeting partners in body-mind-action. Observe their body language and energy, their speech, and finally, their mood or emotions. What might their body language, their tone of voice, and their actions tell you about their energy? How about their language? Which energy represents the tone of their voice and the tone of their words? Finally, observe what mood or emotion they may be displaying. Do they seem happy, enthusiastic, or excited as in being in a Light Energy, or do they seem like they are in Heavy Energy where they are trying to be realistic in their conversation? Are they projecting Inviting Energy and asking a lot of question, while being sincerely interested in what you bring to the table? Conversely, are they more interested in pushing their perspective or ideas and just want others to agree with what they are saying?

Whatever their energy might be, simply observe the energy that you are experiencing.

3. Connect with their energy

    Once you identify the energy you see in your conversation partner, connect with them at their level. Adopt the same energy as they are displaying. Adopting the same energy as they are projecting allows for a natural flow of energy in the room without any unnecessary turmoil. By matching with their energy, you can begin to let them feel that you are present with them in the room. This will raise their sense of safety, even before you speak a word. It's extremely important in this step to understand that matching their energy does not mean matching their behaviour or agreeing with what they are saying. Simply practice projecting the same energy as your partner and nothing else.

4. Engage and empathize

    Once you adopt the same energy as your partner, use empathy to build a stronger connection with your partner. Understand their thoughts, actions, and feelings and speak to those. A fantastic technique here is that of summarizing. Once your partner finishes speaking, engage with what your partner was saying by creating a brief summary of what you think they are saying and feeling. For example, 'If I hear you correctly, this is what you are saying . . . Is that correct?' Try to create a summary that is as short as possible. A shorter summary is a more powerful way of showing how engaged you are with what they are saying. Utilizing this technique will help your partner feel like they are being heard and understood. As they begin to feel more comfortable, their energy projection will begin to shift more towards neutral. Remember, at this point, you do not need to agree with your partner, simply let them know and feel that you are listening deeply to what they are bringing to the conversation.

5. Re-posture

    Finally, once you have connected and engaged with them in their energy, you can begin to gently move with them into a more desirable energy state that might be more suited for a more constructive conversation. A powerful technique in this case is to simply ask whether your partner is open to exploring different perspectives. If the answer is yes, begin to shift your energy back to neutral. Slow down your breathing, relax your body, and slow down your speech. Move yourself through neutral into the desired energy and make sure your partner is joining you. For example, if your desire is to take them into Light Energy, start smiling more and crack a joke or two. Lighten the mood and see if your partner is reciprocating. On the other hand, if you want to move them from being too light and bubbly to more Determined Energy, move through neutral and start asking more serious, action oriented questions to get them into the Determined Energy and so on.

So, there you have it! The formula to deliberately shifting your energy using the five energies starts with being acutely self-aware. Once there, shifting your energy into neutral will help give you the power of choice to then shift into any of the other energies. The more practiced you become at this skill, the more you will be able to start using this to help your people shift their energies, so that they too can become more effective at everything they do. In the next and final chapter, let's take a look at how you can turn your energy practice into an effective daily habit.

Chapter 15

Getting Started Using the Five Tai Chi Principles of Leadership

As I've highlighted a number of times throughout this book, I found many answers to my own life challenges through the practice of martial arts, and for that reason, I also find myself applying many of the lessons from martial arts to my leadership consulting and executive coaching practice.

A number of years ago, I was asked to conduct a leadership tai chi workshop for a pharmaceutical company, during one of their quarterly leadership conferences. The global leadership team of this organization would come together every three months to share with the other global leaders, what each region was doing to meet and exceed performance demands. This quarter, however, things were going to be different, and the CEO of the company knew he needed a fresh approach to this conference. That's when he thought of me.

A few weeks prior to the leadership conference, the regional Human Resources Director of this organization reached out to me to ask if I could meet up with her and the CEO to discuss the option of running an one-day workshop for these global leaders, while they were all at the global conference. Of course, I happily agreed, and a few days later, I met with them in Singapore at their regional office.

Walking into the reception, I did my usual 'test the weather' screening and took a moment to feel the energy in the building. At the reception, the energy seemed a little gloomy. Even though the reception was designed to look extremely classy, and the receptionists seemed very professional, the atmosphere seemed almost sterile. It was as if the receptionists had no personality of its own.

After a few minutes, the Human Resources Director hurried in to greet me. She looked a little frazzled and her breathing was very shallow. As I observed her approaching me, she looked like she was projecting Determined Energy in her approach, but not in a confident and conscious way. Her frazzled nature and her hurried approach made me feel like she was someone who naturally preferred to be in Inviting Energy, or maybe even Light Energy, but due to external circumstances found herself in unconscious Determined Energy. Keeping that observation to myself, I followed her to the conference room where I was to meet with her and the CEO of the company.

Once we were comfortable in the conference room, the CEO joined us with his executive assistant. He had a very different energy from the Human Resources Director. He was more poised and grounded. He moved in a very deliberate manner and was quite soft spoken. The impression that I got from him was that his energy projection was Heavy Energy.

Without much small talk, the CEO began to inform me that the company was about to undergo a massive reorganization, where offices in certain countries were going to be closed and the business is to be consolidated, using Singapore as a hub for the Asia region. The plan was not only to do this in Asia, but in every region globally. What this meant was that a lot of people were going to be retrenched, but on the upside, a lot of people were also going to be hired in the new offices as they were rolling out this reorganization plan. The CEO told me that at this point, the only people who knew about this in Singapore were himself, his assistant, and the Human Resources Director. His plan was to use the quarterly leadership conference to inform his leadership team. His intention was to disclose his reorganization plan on the first day of the conference, and then to spend the rest of the conference working out a rollout plan with his team.

I couldn't help but wonder what type of emotional burden the Human Resources Director must have been bearing, knowing what was going to come, but not being able to share her thoughts or concerns with anyone until after the quarterly leadership conference.

Thinking about this, I also wondered how the CEO's leadership team was going to react to the news on the first day of the conference. I asked the CEO, how he thought his leadership team would respond to the news initially. He sat for a moment quietly and then told me in a very matter of fact way, 'They'll understand … They have no choice … This is going to happen regardless of what they think.' Thinking about this, I asked the CEO if it would serve his team if they had an opportunity to learn how to process the big news of the organizational change in a positive and constructive way that would help them transition emotionally into strategy mode. He agreed!

I then suggested that we kick off the meeting with one of my leadership workshops called 'Leadership Tai Chi'. Leadership Tai Chi teaches leaders who to utilize the five, fundamental tai chi principles to maintain composure and energy in mind-body-action, even during times of perceived chaos. The CEO loved the idea of approaching this challenge in a holistic way.

As agreed, we started the quarterly conference with the Leadership Tai Chi workshop. During the workshop, we did a combination of physical and mental exercises in different emotional scenarios, so the leadership team could learn to regulate their own emotional reactions in a way that would keep them level-headed, no matter what the situation was. One of the exercises we practiced was how to present difficult news to a team or employee. In this exercise, I taught the team how to pause periodically to give people the opportunity to mentally process the news. During these pauses, the leadership team learned to find their neutral and Inviting Energy by shifting their attention away from the news and to their bodies, much like we have practiced in this book.

At the end of the workshop, the CEO stepped up in front of his leadership team and commenced with his big announcement. While he was sharing the announcement, the CEO used the technique of pausing periodically so he could give himself and his team an opportunity to re-establish their balance. Following his example, the team also practiced reconnecting with their neutral and inviting energies during the pauses. By the end of the announcement, the CEO looked around at his team, then looked at me, and asked, 'So what do you guys think?' After a few seconds, the first team member spoke up and said, 'I am so grateful we did this workshop together before you told us. Even though this is a lot to digest, I feel surprisingly calm about the whole thing.' The team went on to spend the next few days working out a strategy for the reorganization plan. Throughout each of the days, the team kept practicing the exercises they had learned on the first day. By the end of the conference, the team had achieved the CEO's objective of developing a strategy that ultimately lead to the successful implementation of the reorganization plan.

A few weeks later, the Human Resources Director reached out to me again to thank me for the work I did with the team and she mentioned to me, how much anxiety she was feeling prior to the workshop. However, after the workshop, she was able to let go of the anxiety and replace anxious energy with inviting and Light Energy. Even though there was a lot of hard work to be done and a lot of tough conversations to take place with the employees, she was still able to continue with her daily practice of the five energies. She wanted to convey to me that using the five tai chi principles really helped her stay on track, despite the chaos that she was experiencing at work.

The reason why I felt compelled to tell this real life story is because these challenges occur every single day in organizations as well as for individuals. No matter how much you promise yourself that you want to learn any new habit, such as the daily practice of the five energies, life may have different plans for you. Your organization may turn upside down, like in the case study above, or you may get promoted. For all we know, there could be another pandemic, or something might happen that could affect your health. No matter what it is, there are always going to be possible situations in your life that can derail a desire to practice learning something new.

For that reason, I want to share with you the five principals of leadership tai chi, so you can use them to help you get started with putting the five energies into daily practice and create a long-term habit that will offer you many great rewards in life.

Principle 1: Relax, remain calm

Tai Chi application

In a combat situation, where adrenalin and cortisol flood our bodies and brains with the purpose of making us stronger during the fight-or-flight response, our bodies and minds get tensed. Even though this may have an evolutionary advantage, there is also a disadvantage. When we are tensed, our movements become rigid, and our minds focus on escaping the threat, rather than on strategies to overcome the challenge ahead.

However, when we can train ourselves to remain relaxed and override that primal temptation to be tense, our bodies are able to move faster and be more agile, while our minds are able to think of winning strategies, thus putting us at an advantage.

Leadership application

In leadership, we often find ourselves in challenging situations multiple times per day. These challenges can be situations like having an uncomfortable conversation, giving feedback to a colleague, receiving an unreasonable request from a boss or team member, and so on.

Our ability to remain relaxed and agile during times of challenge enables our brains to maintain a broader perspective so that we can come up with many more suitable options, rather than responding with an emotional knee-jerk reaction against the perceived threat.

Remaining calm and relaxed during times of perceived threat also has a calming effect on the people around us, who in turn relax and inject calmness into their surroundings, and as such, results in a more agile and resilient organization.

Five Energies practice

Learning something new can feel strange, demanding, and, sometimes, even stressful. Think about the time when you first learned how to ride a bike, drive a car, or perhaps learned how to play a musical instrument. In all likelihood, your first attempt wasn't very graceful. The grace and elegance that came after many hours of practice happened only because you spent many hours practicing. When practicing the five energies, you will likely feel very strange too. Initially, the exercises won't feel graceful, and you may even feel a little embarrassed. This is absolutely normal and is to be expected. If this happens, accept the fact that these movements are going to feel clumsy. Instead of trying to fight the uncomfortable feeling, simply relax your body, slow down your breathing, and calm your mind, and then try again. Each time you feel the tension growing inside you, shift yourself back to relaxing.

When I first started learning tai chi, I really struggled with the ability to relax. I learned through practice that taking a step back to relax is not just critical in becoming a better martial artist, but also a metaphor for life. When tension hits you, simply relax. It has worked miracles for me, for my coaching, and in my martial arts. It will for you too.

Principle 2: Separate yin from yang—pause before you act

Tai Chi application

While practicing the many movements of a tai chi sequence, each movement is executed in an extremely deliberate and precise way. To the regular public, it may look like the movements are flowing from one into the other, but in reality, the flow that you see is a shift from inaction into action and then back into inaction. It's the flow of energy moving back and forth from inaction into action that creates the appearance of flow in this sequence. The reason why the deliberate separation from inaction into action, and then back into inaction looks like such effortless flow is because the phase of inaction is not passive, as one might think. The phase of inaction between actions is utilized by the practitioner to put the body into the most ideal position to allow for the most effective execution of the following action. In fact, that moment of inaction, no matter how small or insignificant it may seem, is actually more important than the action itself, because without it, the action that follows would not be effective.

Leadership application

In times of challenge, it can be tempting for the leadership team to respond reactively with an attempt to overcome the problem as quickly as possible, so that business can continue as usual. One example could be the surgical removal of employees or departments to minimize cost during times of financial decline. Even though such actions maybe appropriate in some circumstances, in others they could cause serious damage to the organization in the long run.

The tai chi approach to overcoming challenges or fixing problems would be to lengthen the pause between the problem and the reaction. During this pause, we can take a deep breath and relax to clear our minds. Just like in practicing tai chi, the pause after a problem presents itself is more important than the actual reaction that follows. During this pause, while we take time to relax and catch our breaths, we can give ourselves permission to think about all the possible scenarios and consequences. We can then shift energy and move ourselves into Inviting Energy and seek suggestions from the other team members or mentors around us. By deliberately utilizing the pause, we will likely come up with a solution or plan of action that will have a much greater impact than if we simply reacted to the problem right away.

Five Energies practice

As you start practicing the five energies exercises and techniques, it may be tempting to jump straight in and try everything at the same time. You may find yourself enthusiastically wanting to use the N.I.C.E.R. model on people you struggle to communicate with. You may feel tempted to jump straight into projecting energy, without doing the actual exercises. This form of impatience is extremely normal. It's always tempting to try out something new with the hope that it will immediately produce different results.

If you find yourself a little impatient with this, remember this second principle. Take a moment to step back and pause. Give yourself time to practice the five energies exercises first. When it comes to the N.I.C.E.R. model, start with just one letter per week. On week one, practice being in Neutral Energy. Once shifting into Neutral Energy begins to feel more natural, practice investigating by observing the energies of people around you. Take your time and just practice being in Neutral Energy, and while in Neutral Energy observing others. Remember, the characteristic of being in Neutral Energy is that your mind is silent, your body is balanced, and you take no action. Observing others while in Neutral Energy means that you can observe others without any judgement. Be patient with this process. It does take practice, so give yourself permission to take long pauses between your stages of development.

Additionally, just like in the case study at the beginning of this chapter, whether you are working on a project, solving problems, giving a presentation, or participating in a very important meeting, lengthening the pauses between actions, comments, or presentation topics gives everyone in the room more time to think. As the leader, practice lengthening the pauses in your conversations, presentations, and meetings, and see how that changes the dynamics of the meeting, your project work, or your presentation.

Principle 3: Keep your back straight and your head high

Tai Chi application

Keeping our spines long and our heads upright enable us to move efficiently without losing balance. Because tai chi is practiced in a relaxed state, it is critical to be able to maintain balance. Without balance, not only do our movements become less effective, but without balance, energy in the body can't flow freely. Furthermore, as our bodies fatigue during practice, we may begin to lose control of our posture. Our posture muscles that keep us in an upright position fatigue during prolonged periods of practicing stances and techniques. As fatigue begins to take over the body and the posture muscles begin to weaken, we can notice slouching of the shoulders. As the posture weakens, so too does the biomechanical effectiveness of any techniques. Even during fatigue, it is critical to maintain balance and keep the head high so energy can continue to flow effectively through the body.

Leadership application

Neuroscience is confirming that how leaders carry themselves greatly influence the mental and physical health of those in their direct environment. In times of challenge, if the leader displays a posture of exhaustion and defeat, such as slouching and hanging his/her head low, the members of the team undergo a number of neurochemical and hormonal changes that not only affect their outlook on the crisis, but also increase their blood pressure and alter their health status.

In other words, how the leader carries himself or herself has a direct influence on the health of the organization, both in the short term and in the long term. Therefore, the ability to keep our heads up, our attitudes positive, and spines long is an essential skill in leadership. Interestingly, self-awareness and self-control are also the pillars of emotional intelligence required in transformational leadership.

Five Energies practice

As I mentioned earlier, keeping your back straight and your head up promote energy flow through the body. No matter what energy you want to project, determined, inviting, light, heavy, and Neutral Energy are all best projected when in an upright posture.

Whenever we learn any new skills, the likelihood of applying that skill perfectly on the first day is very small. Mastering any skill takes practice, lots of practice. The same holds true for the five Energies. Many people, when practicing a new behaviour or skill, become discouraged if they don't see incredible results or growth right away.

With that discouragement comes a change in posture. If you've ever seen anyone who has become discouraged, you would likely see their heads drop and their shoulders slouch. Just like when practicing actual tai chi, this change in posture will immediately result in a reduction of energy flow through the body.

If you find yourself becoming discouraged or frustrated when progress isn't as fast as you would like, remember that simply keeping your head up and back straight will already make a difference in the energy pathways of your body. Keeping your head up and your back straight, even when you are feeling discouraged, is a practice that you can feel proud of.

Principle 4: Pretty lady wrists—be elegant

Tai Chi application

Performing techniques while appearing soft and elegant is a characteristic of tai chi. This softness spreads from the centre of the body and extends all the way through the arms and wrists to the fingertips. For energy to flow freely, all joints must be in an open position. For that reason, the wrist should typically not be bent, nor should it be rigid. It should be open and straight, giving the appearance of pretty lady wrists.

Interestingly, the appearance of softness is, in fact, an illusion. Softness is the vessel that enables energy to flow freely from the centre of the body to the fingertips. It is a state of readiness to enable the martial artist to strike with extreme speed when required. Much like the snake that lies in a coiled position, it appears to be resting, when in fact it is ready to strike instantly and precisely.

Leadership application

Energy management is an essential skill for today's leaders. In the hectic lives of today's busy executives, managing energy is not a simple task. With so many distractions and changes, it can be extremely tempting to expend too much of our energy on one challenge and thus finding ourselves running on empty when we might need it for others.

By applying the same principle of softness and elegance in our daily lives as tai chi practitioners do, it is possible to minimize unnecessary energy expenditure. By keeping an open, authentic posture, and remaining as relaxed as possible through many of our tasks and challenges in a day, we can assume the position of elegance while simultaneously being ready to act swiftly and with precision, where required.

Another advantage is that an open and authentic posture displays a greater level of approachability and arouses trust in those who seek our leadership, while simultaneously, acting with precision helps us ward off unnecessary conflicts and overcome the necessary challenges with grace.

Five Energies practice

As you begin to learn how to use the five energies, you may initially find yourself in situations where you inadvertently choose the wrong energy projection. You may also find that your ability to read the energy in others might not always be accurate, at the beginning.

If you find yourself in a situation where you applied the wrong energy, or you find yourself reading someone else's energy wrong, you may find yourself in a bit of an embarrassing situation that could leave you feeling out of balance.

In that moment, don't become discouraged. Simply take an elegant step back and shift your energy back into Neutral Energy, just like we practiced in the previous chapters. From there, readjust yourself in the situation by shifting to a more appropriate energy. Readjusting your energy will help you maintain your composure and balance in this situation.

Principle 5: Move from your hips—be centred

Tai Chi application

When learning new movements in tai chi, it can be extremely tempting to focus outward on how our hands and feet are moving. However, true power resides not in the hands or feet. All power in tai chi is generated from the centre of gravity in our bodies, our hips. What this means is that the focus of the tai chi practitioner should not be from the outside in, or from the extremities to the centre, but rather from the centre of the body to the extremities.

Leadership application

When we lead, it can also be extremely tempting to focus outward. Undesirable cultures, disengaged employees, underperforming teams, and how those factors are affecting the business are just a few examples of an outward to inward focus.

However, if we were to utilize the tai chi approach, the focus should be from the inside to the outside. In this case, asking the question, 'How is my energy, behaviour, or mindset contributing to the manifestation of this undesirable culture, disengaged employees, or underperforming team?' The next question could then be: 'How can a shift in my behaviour or attitude help improve the status quo?' This form of leadership will likely produce much greater success rather than attempting to force or influence the behaviour of others, using the outward to inward focus approach.

Five Energies practice

As you begin practicing the new skills that are in this book, you may also find yourself tempted to start with an outward to inward focus, meaning that you might think of how you can use your energy to respond to the energy projected by the other people in the room.

Just like in tai chi, finding the centre of your body will enable you to enter the room and the meeting with a much greater sense of power and control. Instead of thinking how you can use the five energies to influence other people, which is an outside to inside focus, think of what energy you need to bring to the meeting that will put you in a greater sense of balance and self-control and will allow you to shift into any of the energies at will. Of course, this energy is Neutral Energy.

What this means is that the most powerful energy you'd want to master, before any of the other four energies, is Neutral Energy. Your ability to effortlessly shift from, and back into Neutral Energy will give you the power to respond efficiently to any situation you may find yourself in.

Conclusion

As we wrap up this book, remember that nothing in life that is worth something comes easy. Give yourself permission to practice, stumble, and fail often. Hold on to the five Tai Chi principles of staying relaxed, pausing often, keeping your head up and spine straight, staying elegant through your practice, and remember that your power comes when you operate from Neutral Energy first.

These principles will help you push yourself through your practice and maintain a rhythm, so that in time you will begin to feel like you are operating with the Energy of a tai chi master in your everyday life.

Final Thoughts

As you've come to the end of this book, I would like to finish off by saying how incredibly proud I am of you for having the courage to practice the five energies. One of my executive coaching mentors, Dr Marshall Goldsmith, taught me that the three most important characteristics of a great leader are courage, humility, and discipline.

I wholeheartedly agree with this statement. For you to have made it this far into this book and practicing all of the exercises as they were presented, you would have demonstrated that you too possess these three qualities. It took you courage to pick up this book, start reading, and then to start asking yourself some pretty tough questions about how you show up in your work and life. That action of courage shows up when you were able to operate in Determined Energy.

Being able to admit to yourself that you have areas in your way of operating that may require some attention takes a great amount of humility and that is not something everyone possesses naturally. Being receptive to the contents of this book and being open to practice a new way of operating can only occur while being in Inviting Energy.

Finally, if you managed to prioritize time and energy to practice the exercises in this book, you demonstrated incredible discipline. Despite the fact that you have a million things going on in your life, you managed to stand your ground, roll up your sleeves, and get the job done. You managed to do this by applying Heavy Energy.

Now, as you move forward with these new skills, have some fun. Don't take yourself or these skills too seriously. Apply some Light Energy in your practice of these new skills and notice how learning in lightness can be extremely invigorating and uplifting.

Finally, it's not a sin to ask for help when practicing these skills. Find people around you who might want to learn these techniques too. That could be just one person, or it could be an entire team. Having a support group will help you to stay on track.

Additionally, consider using a coach if you are not already using one. This framework is intuitive enough for most executive and life coaches to pick up quickly.

Another resource that will help you is my website: www.marceldaane. com. There, you will find lots of resources, including instructional videos, and more information on the five energies assessment.

I wish you all the best and once again, thank you for taking this journey with me.

Acknowledgements

First and foremost, I would like to say thanks to my mother and father for raising me with a strong set of core values that have functioned as a guiding light through my very colourful life, even during times of perceived darkness. To my mom who, through her dedication to justice and equality, helped bring down a white supremacist regime in South Africa and was an incredible inspiration to me at the same time. To my dad, who sadly passed away due to COVID-19 during the pandemic. He showed me every day that there is tremendous strength in being accepting, compassionate, loving. I will miss you always.

Further, I would like to say thank you to the giants on whose shoulders I stand. Without the courage and insight from the amazing teachers in my life, this book would not have been conceptualized. To my martial arts teachers for introducing me to the power of my own energy. To the ancient philosophers whose writings hold truth till today. To my professional teachers, such as the incredible minds at the Neuro-leadership Institute, Newfield Network, and The Strozzi Institute for carving a path ahead of me that helped me formulate the system in this book. To the many great mentors, such as the team at The Coach Partnership in Singapore, Marshall Goldsmith, and Dr Phil Merry for showing me what good looks like in coaching, and finally, to the hundreds of my clients who gave me permission to experiment on them over the years.

I would like to finish with a special note to the two most important people in my life. My beautiful wife, Ursula, and my daughter, Kilani.

are the rocks in my life. Without their loving support, patience, and wisdom, I would not be the person I am today.

I am in your debt!

Thank you all!

Tools for
Your Journey

*"No problem can be solved from the same level
of consciousness that created it."*
Albert Einstein

As you commence on your Five Energies journey toward greater effectiveness, you will need access to resources to expand your consciousness about your health and performance.

The contents of this book are just the beginning. To help you along on the wonderful discovery of your energy, you will need access to in-depth material and all the latest advances in the field.

I also know that people learn differently. This is why I have created a place where you can access the pioneering research, learn new techniques and applications and even get personalized coaching.

Get **FREE** Resources
now at
MarcelDaane.com

Five Energies Online Assessment

Take 7 minutes and try my FREE Five Energies Self-Assessment on my website for a quick overview of your default energy. Want something more comprehensive? Sign up for the Five Energies Leadership 360-degree Assessment or for the comprehensive Five Energies Team Assessment to assess what default energy your team projects.

Keynotes

Book me for a speaking engagement at one of your leadership conferences or events. These keynote addresses deliver a basic and experiential introduction to the numerous factors required for superior performance by executives. The presentation is ideal for a broader audience with minimal time investment, such as during corporate events and leadership retreats.

Workshops

Interested in learning how to apply the Five Energies in a practical setting? Sign up for one of my Five Energies Workshops or book me for an exclusive Five Energies Leadership Workshop in your organization.

Executive Coaching

For a more exclusive approach to attaining superior levels of performance, my Executive Coaching sessions involve deepening your understanding of your Five Energies, followed by a goal-oriented executive coaching methodology to enable new insights, and learning new habits that elevate your capacity as a leader and professional.

Webinars

Join me for a variety of online teaching events that focus on the science and application of The Five Energies.

Blog and Email Newsletters

Sign up for *Marcel's blog* on marceldaane.com, and receive periodic emails that provide the latest news, research, applications, and opinions. You will get lots of free ideas and tools for you and your entire organization.

LinkedIn.com/MarcelDaane

If you are an executive—and even if you are not—connect with Marcel through LinkedIn.

Twitter.com/MarcelDaane

Keep in touch wherever you are by following Marcel's twitter feed. Be the first to know what's going on in the world of Five Energies Leadership.

YouTube.com/MarcelDaane

The online video home of the Five Energies gives you access to dozens of videos on tai chi, Leadership, and of course, The Five Energies.

Join the
Five Energies
Community

Join Marcel Daane, and many thousands of Five Energies enthusiasts. Our community is ever growing and we invite you to join us in our quest to be the best that we can be in all areas of life. Here, we share the latest news, ideas and research, and open up the forum for mindful discussion. Share with us your experiences and get answers to your questions from other Five Energies enthusiasts around the world.

Our community members are committed to their performance and are always seeking ways to upgrade themselves to greater levels of health, well-being, and performance capacity.

Find out more about these resources at MarcelDaane.com